Edinburgh

AN ILLUSTRATED ARCHITECTURAL GUIDE

Compiled by
CHARLES McKEAN
with
DAVID WALKER
for

THE EDINBURGH
ARCHITECTURAL ASSOCIATION
125TH ANNIVERSARY

Introduction by
Colin McWilliam

© Charles McKean
ISBN 0-9501462-4-2

Designed by James Forbes and Charles McKean
Cover by James Forbes

Published by

RIAS Publications, 15 Rutland Square, Edinburgh EH1 2BE
with the support of Edinburgh District Council

Printed by Lindsay & Co. Ltd.

How to use this Guide

Organisation

This guide is divided into two sections for the convenience of the visitor:

Section 1: *The Old and New Towns of Edinburgh,* arranged on a geographical basis. Although this method does not give a clear visual picture of how architecture developed through the centuries, it makes a much handier Guide for the pedestrian. The walking tours approximate to the following pattern:

(a) The Royal Mile
(b) The Cowgate to Lothian Road and Tollcross
(c) Tollcross to the University and the South Side
(d) The New Town
(e) The Eastern New Town
(f) The Northern New Town
(g) The Western New Town

Section 2: *Edinburgh beyond the New Town:* beginning with short guides to those outlying communities that still retain an architectural coherence —pre-eminently Leith. The exclusion of a village—e.g. Corstorphine— indicates that there is little surviving homogeneous character, despite the existence of one or two outstanding monuments. The villages are followed by a chronological guide to the remaining Edinburgh buildings of note. The area covered makes it impossible to arrange a sensible geographical pattern to these buildings. Furthermore, it is only in the chronological section that the patterns of architectural change become apparent.

Layout

The text has been written as a series of notes, rather than an extended architectural or historical description. Where possible, each entry is laid out in the following fashion:

The name of the building (or its identifiable address), together with the street address; followed by that of the designer or architect (where identifiable): followed by the date (usually but not invariably that of the design, and not of the completion of construction).

Access

Although many buildings in this *Guide* are public and thereby easily accessible, a large number are privately owned and used. Inclusion of a building in this Guide does not imply a right of access, and readers are asked to respect the owner's privacy.

Photographic Credits

Most of the photographs in this book have been taken or collected specially for this Guide and the name of the source is shown next to each photograph, with the exception of those photographs submitted by the architects themselves. We should particularly like to thank the following people for their great help in providing illustrations:

The Royal Commission on the Ancient and Historical Monuments of Scotland, for photographs on pages 19, 21, 22, 23, 30, 31, 33, 36, 37, 38, 40, 51, 52, 58, 63, 67, 69, 71, 76, 77, 78, 80, 83, 86, 87, 90, 93, 94, 95, 97, 98, 104; The Property Services Agency for photographs on pages 42, 53, 64, 98; Robert Hurd & Partners, who kindly lent their photo-grapher/designer Shona Adam for the purpose of taking some of the photographs in this Guide, on pages 16, 18, 24, 27, 35, 39, 48, 49, 53, 80, 91, 94.

The City of Edinburgh Museums and Galleries for the drawing on page 28; John and Scott Robertson for photographs on pages 16, 32, 33, 38, 87, 98, 99, 100, 102, 103, 107; Charles McKean for photographs on pages 13, 19, 24, 26, 31, 32, 34, 37, 39, 40, 50, 51, 52, 53, 57, 59, 61, 62, 63, 66, 67, 68, 69, 70, 75, 76, 77, 78, 81, 82, 83, 87, 88, 89, 90, 91, 92, 93, 96, 100, 101, 102, 103, 105, 106, 107, 110, 113; Joe Rock for photographs on pages 18, 47, 48, 49, 50, 51, 54, 57, 59, 60, 61, 65, 95, 96, 97, 99; Inglis Stevens, photographers, for photographs on pages 41, 43, 54, 55, 66, 79, 84, 85, 99, 104; and White House Photography for photographs on pages 69, 71. We are also indebted to White House Photography and to Inglis Stevens for other substantial, photographic services.

For reasons of variety we have used illustrations from older documents including: *The Baronial and Ecclesiastical Architecture of Scotland,* by R. W. Billings (1847-52); *Theatrum Scotia* by John Slezer (1693); *The Castellated and Domestic Architecture of Scotland,* by David McGibbon and Thomas Ross; *Edinburgh, a Sketchbook,* by J. G. Thornby (1910) courtesy of Charles McKean. Also included are reproductions of drawings or photographs kindly lent by the National Monuments Record, the City of Edinburgh District Council, John L. Paterson of the Edinburgh College of Art; the RIAS Library and Drawings Collection; the Edinburgh Architectural Association Library; the Wallace Trust; the Heriot Trust; I. Fisher; the National Gallery of Modern Art; Scottish Colourfoto Laboratories; Edinburgh Central Libraries; R. Emerson; and the Royal Scottish Academy.

Acknowledgements

This Guide had its origins in the Edinburgh Architectural Association Guide first published in 1964 and revised in 1969. The original Guide owed much to John Reid and to Colin McWilliam as compilers. This new Guide, once more commissioned by the Edinburgh Architectural Association, has been compiled by Charles McKean, (solely to whom can any inaccuracies or erractic value judgements be charged), with the enormous assistance of David Walker, Principal Inspector of Historic Buildings, the Historic Buildings Council, and John Gifford and Colin McWilliam, together with the **Buildings of Scotland** Research Unit, whose impending volume on Edinburgh is eagerly awaited.

The Guide could not be in the form it is today without the support and encouragement of John D. Robertson, the appointed representative of the Edinburgh Architectural Association, the Royal Commission on Ancient and Historical Monuments of Scotland, particularly Miss Catherine Cruft and Mr. Ian Gow; Stuart Harris, Depute City Architect for the City of Edinburgh, Miss Elizabeth Cumming, Mr. and Mrs. John D. Richards, and Messrs Stuart Renton, John Reid, Michael Mannings, Chris Watkins, and the many architects who have submitted details of their buildings. John Bartholomew and Son Ltd kindly provided originals of the maps, which were prepared by John Robertson; the cover design is that of James Forbes; and production was by Charles McKean.

Exceptional thanks are due to the City of Edinburgh District Council for their financial support for this project; and to the staff of the Royal Incorporation of Architects in Scotland, and to Mrs. Catherine Nicholson for typing.

How d'ye like Edinburgh?
It is a dream of a great genius, said I.
Well done, said Sir Walter.
B. R. Haydon, recalling his meeting
with Sir Walter Scott in 1820.

INTRODUCTION

Colin McWilliam.

Author of **Scottish Townscape** and **Lothian,** the first volume in the
projected **Buildings of Scotland** series.

Old Town, New Town, outlying villages absorbed, and estates overbuilt
by later development. Many cities have the same pattern of growth, but
none shows it so clearly. Most cities are in some way special; Edinburgh in
its own way is more special than others.

What does one notice? First the extraordinary site of the central area—a
group of volcanic hills sticking up from the coastal plain at its narrowest
point, where the Pentland range comes closest to the Forth, and thus
commanding the entry to Scotland (the line of the A1 and the railway).
The Castle Rock (138m.) was fortified by the Picts and then became the
starting point for a linear settlement descending the tail which had been left
by glacial action to the east. Edinburgh probably became a Royal (i.e.
commercial) Burgh in the 12th century under David I, and it was he who
granted the burgh of Canongate (**gait** meaning street), further down the
ridge, to the Canons of Holyrood Abbey, whose mediaeval church still
stands by the royal palace of Holyroodhouse. The principal streets of the
two burghs, formerly separated by the Netherbow Port (gate) together
forms what has been known since the 16th century as the Royal Mile. The
surrounding terrain posed problems for later expansion, and the result is
startingly romantic even where the buildings and layout are most
doggedly classical.

Then there is the stone. At first it was harled rubble, except for the
grandest buildings, and this continued to be used for artisan tenements
well into the 19th century. But mainly it consists of huge masses and
expanses of ashlar in one-foot or larger courses, from the sandstone
quarries to the west of the city, notably Craigleith and Hailes. Its yellow or
white has weathered to a silver grey, challenged in the late 19th century by
red sandstone from Dumfries-shire, and now by the effects of more or less
successful 'stone cleaning.'

Another factor is discipline. Structural standards were enforced from the
start by the Dean of Guild (replaced since 1975 by the Director of Building
Control). Other architectural standards also came under his jurisdiction
till 1947, since when they have been increasingly the concern of the
planning authority. But a much more important part has been played by
the Scottish system of feudal control, under which the feudal superior (e.g.
the owner of an estate selling ground for development) was able to lay
down rules for use and design, and enforce them for ever. The system had
lapsed in most parts of the city, but its orderly results survive. The
completeness of a formal Georgian scheme and the consistency of
character in a suburban villa development are an indication of how well
the superiors and their architects calculated the demand for these types of
accommodation.

Part of John Slezer's view of Edinburgh from the north 1693. Clearly visible are the steeples of St. Giles and the old steeple of the Tron. Trinity College Church and the Nor' Loch are in the foreground

In architectural style, the impression is of conformity and scholarship, constantly fired with originality. A great generation of late Georgian architects established the city's neoclassical image and belatedly justified the nickname 'Modern Athens.' Archibald Elliot died in 1823 but Robert Reid, Gillespie Graham, Thomas Hamilton and William Playfair lived and worked into the 1850s so that there is no sudden break between Georgian and Victorian. William Burn moved to London in 1844, but his sometime partner David Bryce became the giant among mid-Victorian Edinburgh architects. In Bryce's office many of the outstanding later Victorian performers were trained. Rowand Anderson, the most brilliant of all, was Bryce's partner as a young man, and among Anderson's apprentices was Robert Lorimer. Alan Reiach worked for Lorimer, and the late Robert Matthew was the son of Lorimer's partner. There are many such successions and dynasties, going back to the master masons of the city and the crown, to the Mylnes and the Adams.

Old Edinburgh has its mediaeval burgh kirk (the High Kirk of St. Giles), which was subdivided after the Reformation, stabilized in a late Georgian Gothic box, and internally restored to something like a 'cathedral' image in the late 19th century. It also has a remarkable number of 16th and 17th century merchant's houses, and much plain Georgian infill. Canongate has its 16th century tolbooth (town hall) and Netherlandish 17th century kirk, and its grander houses and tenements are mainly those of the landed nobility. The whole Royal Mile has been heavily developed on its backlands, the tunnel-like pends giving access to narrow closes, many of whose buildings reach a tremendous height as they descend to the slopes to north and south. Victorian redevelopment, in a series of Improvement Acts, deliberately kept up the Old Scots image of the town, and at the end of the century Patrick Geddes supplied infill and restoration whose picturesque quality (e.g. at Ramsay Garden) has till recently been too little appreciated. Post-war rebuilding, mainly in Canongate, has continued the tradition in blander fashion—but much better than the gaps which are the other 20th century contribution. At present (1982) the chief rehabilitation effort is in the Grassmarket, the magnificent space to the south which is reached by way of Victoria Street (one of the many late Georgian road improvements) and a small fragment of the Old West Bow, complete with its old houses.

Large-scale expansion began in the 1760s: to the south George Square, to the north the official New Town, a symmetrical gridiron planned by James Craig in 1766. This First New Town shows the steady development of civic grandeur from the modest houses of St. Andrew Square, along George Street to the aristocratic palace-fronts of Charlotte (intended as St. George's) Square, the late work of Robert Adam. It also shows long terraces with open views to south and north (Princes and Queen Streets). Later additions (monuments, and axially sited buildings like the Royal Scottish Academy on the mound) and even large redevelopments (Victorian banks, hotels and stores) have emphasized the suitability of Craig's layout for this distinctive site.

The title New Town is now given to the whole area of continuous Georgian development—about a square mile in all—from Princes Street to the north, east and west. It consists, in fact, of a series of new towns, separately planned but neatly joined one to another, whose formality is constantly challenged and inflected (except to the west) by the lie of the ground, producing what Professor Hitchcock has called 'the most extensive example of a classical-romantic city in the world.'. To the south, and linked to the centre by the multi-arched South Bridge, past Adam's monumental entry to the University Old Quad, came a more workaday but equally impressive development of great gabled tenements.

Villa developments, which had started in the 18th century in Gayfield Square, are seen at their most compact in Blacket Place, at their most fanciful near the seaside, at Trinity and Portobello. Greenhill Gardens is the prettiest early Victorian area, Grange the most sedate and Merchiston the most imaginative of later Victorian districts. Colinton, in its charming position to the far south-west above the Water of Leith, is the ultimate suburb and produced the ultimate type of suburban dwelling in Lorimer's 'Colinton cottages'—designs of great finesse, but cosy and relaxed.

The Victorian tenement is one of Edinburgh's most memorable—and to the visitor even intimidating—building types. Bay-windowed and corner-turreted, it barged into Bruntsfield scattering Georgian villas right and left, overran Marchmont on the other side of the Meadows, and infiltrated Merchiston, as it did many other suburbs. Comely Bank's late 19th century tenements are plainer, but their downhill enfilade of tall bay windows is brutally effective. Mostly these were for middle-class owners; their artisan counterparts, dreadfully plain or strangely fanciful, are seen on the east side—notably round Easter Road.

Edinburgh's old slums have largely disappeared, though some of the Old Town's distinguished buildings which sank to that status have survived and are being rescued. But they must be remembered as the background to housing enterprises like the Stockbridge 'Colonies,' and the picturesque Well Court in the Dean Village. Inter-war public house began very handsomely (indeed before the Housing Acts) at Northfield, off Willowbrae Road, and maintained a decent standard. So did the more central post-war schemes, like that which replaced the notorious Dumbiedykes, between Holyrood Road and Queen's Park. With unhappy hindsight, it is now clear that the most successful developments have been the most modest and conventional, like the Inch scheme on the way to Gilmerton, and the extensive rebuilding of old Newhaven. Recently the initiative in public (or semi-public) housing has passed to the Housing Associations, which have particularly excelled in rehabilitation; the Lister block in Keir Street/Lauriston Place has been restored with exceptional care.

In the city with such a durable and important past, outstanding buildings of the twentieth century are few in number and sometimes hard to find. The glass curtain wall made its debut in Bread Street before the war, reappeared brilliantly at the Standard Life extension off George Street in the 1950s, and then more controversially in Princes Street. A constant problem in urban infill is how to design a masonry frontage that will not look like a mere parody of the old-style load-bearing wall. Alternative conventions have been worked out at 114 George Street and at a number of offices in St. Andrew Square.

For spectacular industrial architecture one must look outside the centre, e.g. to the King's buildings boilerhouse, the P.O. sorting office and the Gas Board headquarters. Likewise the calm horizontals of the International Style are only seen on outlying sites—mostly in private houses but with immense success at the Royal Commonwealth Pool, which was a turning point in Edinburgh's attitude to modern architecture.

THE OLD AND NEW TOWNS

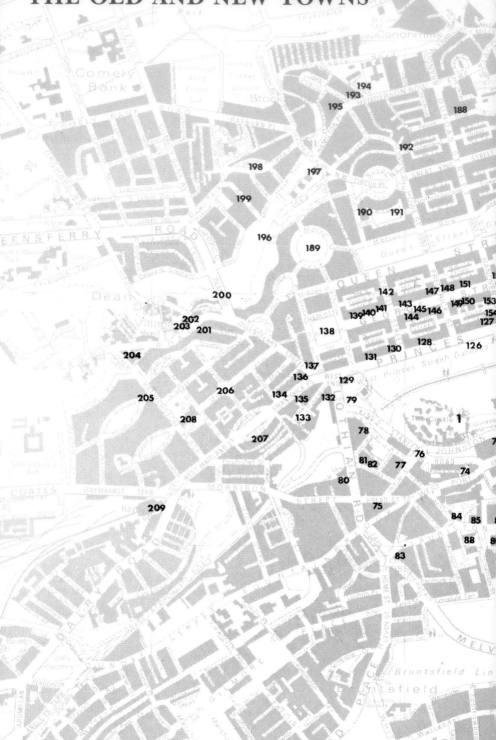

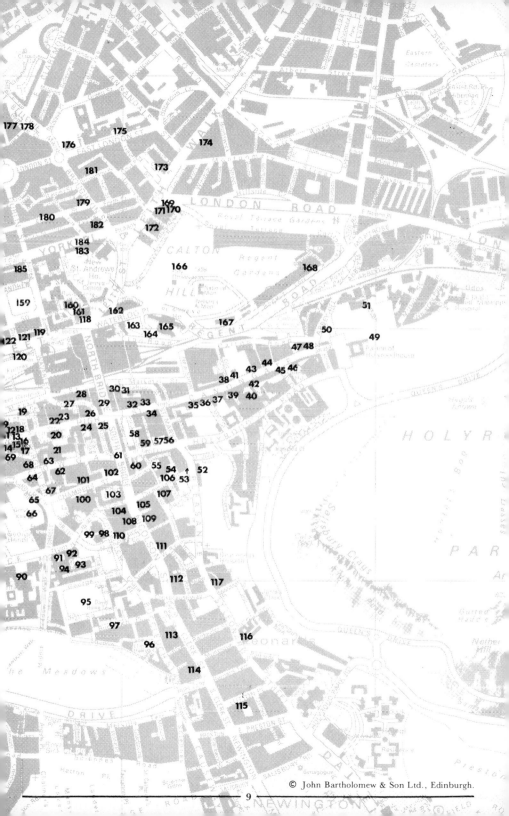

© John Bartholomew & Son Ltd., Edinburgh.

Edinburgh
SECTION ONE

The Old and New Towns

For the convenience of pedestrians this section
is organised as a series of walking tours.

THE ROYAL MILE
THE COWGATE TO TOLLCROSS
THE SOUTH SIDE
THE NEW TOWN
THE EASTERN NEW TOWN
THE NORTHERN NEW TOWN
THE WESTERN NEW TOWN

The Loch-side City: Edinburgh in 1693

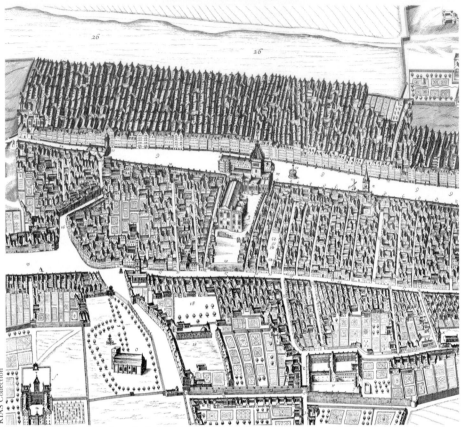

The Royal Mile, drawn by James Gordon of Rothiemay 1647

RIAS Collection

THE ROYAL MILE is the nickname given to the route from Edinburgh Castle to Holyrood Palace, down a volcanic ridge. Properly speaking, it is a conjunction of four streets: Castle Hill, Lawnmarket, High Street and Canongate, from which side routes of lanes and alleys, called closes or wynds, lead off like herring bones from its spine. It has always attracted attention. In 1636 an English traveller, Sir William Brereton, commended the *great street, which I do take to be an English mile long, and is the best paved street with boulder stones that I have seen. This street is the glory and beauty of this city: it is the broadest street . . . and the longest street I have seen. . . . The street, if the houses which are high, and substantially built of stone were not lined on the outside and faced with boards, it were the most stately and graceful street that ever I saw in my life. . .* By the 19th century, the Quality had removed to the New Town, leaving the Old to squalor. In 1847 Hans Christian Andersen observed that *the many side streets off it are narrow, filthy and with six-storey houses; one has to think of the great buildings in the dirty towns of Italy; poverty and misery seem to peep out of the open hatches which normally serve as windows.*

Public conscience finally stimulated the passing of the Old Town Improvement Act which widened many of the old wynds and closes, with the result that fewer historic buildings have survived from the wynds than have from the Royal Mile itself. In 1892 Patrick Geddes initiated, from his University base, a programme for the restoration of old buildings in the Old Town, and their re-occupation by students and University Departments. Geddes wrote *Our large perspective of the upper third of the ridge of old Edinburgh now becomes intelligible as a definite and gradually unifying scheme; not simply for the cleansing and conservation of the historic remains of old Edinburgh, but for the development of this into a collegiate street and city comparable in its way with the magnificent High Street of Oxford and its noble surroundings.* This crucial intervention saved important buildings, principally in the Lawnmarket. After further decay and sporadic rehabilitation in the '30s (such as Acheson House and Huntly House) the City Corporation initiated a post-war policy of restoration and rebuilding in the Canongate under the control of Robert Hurd.

Edinburgh Castle, drawn by John Slezer 1693

McKean

Cannonball House, drawn by McGibbon & Ross 1896

1 EDINBURGH CASTLE

The oldest building in the castle is the diminutive, fortress-like 12th century St. Margaret's Chapel on the summit of the rock, with a fine ornamented chancel arch. East of the Palace yard is the King's lodging where James VI was born in 1566; he ordered the extension of the block in 1615 and here the Honours of Scotland are preserved. South of the yard is the Great Hall, with a timber roof dating from early 16th century, much restored by H. J. Blanc in 1888. On the west is a simple range of buildings (1707), now gutted to form a Museum. West of the Citadel, at a lower level is the Governor's House of 1742 and a magnificent barrack block of 1796 set on a an arcaded basement. The lower portion of Argyll Tower dates from 1574. Most interesting part of the ramparts is the Half-Moon battery built by the Regent Morton around the remains of the large 14th century King David II Tower, which was ruined during the long siege, 1570-1573, when Kirkcaldy of Grange held the Castle for Mary Queen of Scots. The Scottish National Memorial for the First World War was designed by Sir Robert Lorimer. **Guide book available.**

2 CANNONBALL HOUSE, Castle Hill 1630 (south wing).

Large merchant's house whose nickname derives from the cannonball embedded in the west gable. Dormer window inscribed AM MN 1630 (after Alex Mure, an Edinburgh furrier and his wife). Crow-stepped gable facing south; grand, mid 18th century three-gabled street front with raised moulded doorway. Interesting stone guides for sliding shutters at some of the windows.

Ian G Lindsay

Aerial View of the Lawnmarket: The spire is Tolbooth St. John's. Ramsay Garden can be seen on the right
Below: *The Outlook Tower*

3 RAMSAY GARDEN
18th century with 19th century additions

Fantastic, turretted, red and white flats on the edge of the Esplanade incorporating the 18th century octagonal house belonging to the father of the painter, Allan Ramsay.
19th century additions and alterations romantically conceived by Sir Patrick Geddes and executed by S. Henbest Capper, 1892, and Sydney Mitchell, 1893. They were designed to attract University lecturers and professors back to live in the old town., Capper, a pupil of J. L. Pascal at the École des Beaux Arts, was a follower of Geddes.

4 OUTLOOK TOWER, 549 Castle Hill

Bottom storeys 17th century, castellated upper storeys being added 1853 when converted into a Camera Obscura. Adopted by Sir Patrick Geddes 1895-96 as the Outlook Tower and interpretative Centre. Still a Camera Obscura: also a Museum.
Guide book available.

5 BOSWELL'S COURT, 352 Castle Hill
17th century.

A 5-storey tenement with pedimented dormers, crow-stepped gable and moulded doorway with inscription at back. Named after uncle of James Boswell.

Ian G Lindsay

-14-

North facade of the Old Town: reading right to left—
Ramsay Garden, Outlook Tower, Tolbooth St John's,
New College, Free Church Offices, James Court

6 TOLBOOTH ST. JOHN'S CHURCH,
Lawnmarket
James Gillespie Graham, 1842-44.

Built as Victoria Hall for Established Church
General Assembly. Designed in collaboration
with A. W. N. Pugin; soaring Gothic tower
with pinnacles, topped by an octagonal spire.
Inside, a grand staircase leads to a galleried
auditorium, with fine single-span ribbed
plaster vault, and intricate woodwork
executed by William Nixon to Pugin's
designs. It is said that Pugin met Graham
when the latter helped him after a shipwreck
near Leith. The Pugin influence brings to life
an otherwise unexceptional building.

7 MILNE'S COURT, 513-523 Lawnmarket
Robert Mylne, 1690

Earliest essay in large courtyard planning in
the Old Town by the man responsible for
much of the work at Holyrood. The west side
has been demolished and a large part of the
east side rebuilt. The eight storey north block
is entered through moulded doorway at third
floor level from courtyard; six storey,
octagonal staircase tower projecting from east
side. Restored as Edinburgh University Halls
of Residence by Ian G. Lindsay and Partners,
1968.

8 NEW COLLEGE and ASSEMBLY HALL,
Lawnmarket
William Playfair, 1846-50.

Distinctly foreign, Tudor collegiate
development set on northern axis of Tolbooth
St. John's spire, its twin-towered and orielled
gatehouse à la Oxbridge dominating the main
elevation facing Princes Street. Quadrangle,
with two octagonal towers on south side.
Assembly Hall on north by David Bryce,
1858-59, partly rebuilt by J. M. Dick Peddie
in 1901. Rainy Hall to east by Sydney
Mitchell, 1899.

9 FREE CHURCH OF SCOTLAND COLLEGE and OFFICES,
North Bank Street
David Cousin, 1858-60

Soaring neo-Jacobean fantasy, partly
incorporating James Brownhill's James Court
Buildings (see below) with concatenation of
towers, turrets and dormers. Impressive
Presbytery Hall within.

Milne's Court, drawn by Ian Marshall

10 3 and 5 JAMES COURT, 501 Lawnmarket
Partly 1725-7.

Erected by James Brownhill, a speculator and
builder, after whom it was named. The Court
became the most fashionable flats in the 18th
century city, in one of which Boswell
entertained Dr. Johnson in 1773. Nos. 3 and
5 were picturesquely recast as part of
Geddes's 1892 improvement scheme,
(probably to designs by Henbest Capper, his
spoor recognisable from the use of yellow
wash and red tiles.) No. **6 and 11-14 North
Bank Street,** 1725-7, forms a gaunt masonry
cliff facing Princes Street; the interior
reconstructed by J. & F. Johnston and
Partners, 1981-82.

11 GLADSTONE'S LAND,
483-489 Lawnmarket
1617-20.

Frontage by Thomas Gledstanes, merchant,
grafted on to a house of earlier date, the
original front of which can be seen at the back
of the first floor painted room. Narrow six
storey tenement of ashlar, two gables facing
the street and customary curved external
staircase. They were not always popular.
About 1500, the poet William Dunbar wrote:
Your fore-stairis makis your housses mirk (dark);
and in 1689, Thomas Morer considered *their
stairs are unsightly and inconvenient: for, being built
out of the street for the service of every storey, they are
sometimes so steepy, narrow and fenceless that it
requires care to go up and down for fear of falling.*
The building is notable for preservation of
ground floor arcading, once common in Scots
towns; now giving a slightly bandy-legged
appearance. (Arcades were later re-
introduced into the post-war restoration of the
Canongate by Robert Hurd.) Fine internal
features such as ceilings and walls painted in
tempera with abstract patterns of fruit,
flowers, birds and arabesques, and original
fireplaces. Restored in 1935 by Sir Frank
Mears; and again in 1980 by Robert Hurd
and Partners, as a 17th century merchant's
shop and house for the National Trust for
Scotland. **Guide book available.**

12 LADY STAIR'S HOUSE, 477 Lawnmarket
Completed 1622.

Free standing rubble mansion with hexagonal
projecting stair tower, originally standing in a
narrow close and shorn of later extensions
north and south. Romantically recreated
(from 1895) by George Shaw Aitken with
quasi-English mediaeval interior for Lord
Rosebery at behest of Patrick Geddes. Now a
Literary Museum to Scott, Burns and
Stevenson. **Guide book available.**
Note also: **Blackie House,** 17th century,
oriels, red roof, dormers etc., added 1894 for
University Hall reconstruction which retained
much original interior work. Returned to flats
by Robert Hurd 1949-50.

Gladstone's Land

Lady Stair's House

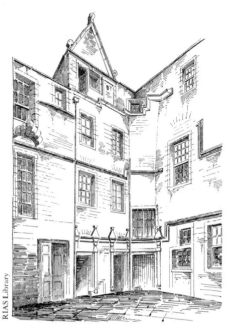

Baillie McMorran's House, drawing by McGibbon & Ross 1896

RIAS Library

13 BURNS LAND
451-463 Lawnmarket
S. Henbest Capper, 1893.

Orielled and gabled tenement fronting Wardrop's Court, with decorative blue dragons flanking the entrance pend. Huntly House type gables slice across the top of the curiously roughcast bays. Scots in scale: English Queen Anne in detail.

14 BAILIE MACMORRAN'S HOUSE,
Riddle's Close, 322 Lawnmarket
16th century.

An arched pend leads through to Riddle's Court, whose inner stair tower is dated 1726 over doorway, a three storey 17th century building with string courses forming the south side. A further arched pend leads to second court containing 16th century Bailie MacMorran's House, scene of a Royal Banquet in 1598. This second court sports pilasters, corbels and string courses. The interiors retain magnificent ceilings, fine panelling and plasterwork. According to historians MacGibbon and Ross *the courtyard of this house is one of the best preserved examples of old domestic architecture remaining in Edinburgh.* Restored in 1893 as University Hall and flats by S. Henbest Capper as a key part of Patrick Geddes Old Town programme, and again in 1964 for Edinburgh Corporation as further Education Rooms by J. Wilson Paterson.

15 312-328 LAWNMARKET
1726 and 1752

One of the Royal Mile's best 18th century frontages: a six storey procession of regular windows sixteen bays long, capped by six curvilinear double gables. The eastern half, of ashlar masonry was internally reconstructed as the Carnegie Library by James Shearer; the western half, rubble built, was restored for Edinburgh Corporation by J. Wilson Paterson in 1959 as flats.

16 BRODIE'S CLOSE
and BUCHANAN'S CLOSE,
298-310 Lawnmarket
17th century.

Quainter than its grander, western neighbour, the street front is dominated by a picturesque array of gables and dormer windows, and the sturdy arched entrance to the pend at the centre. The wing on west side of Brodie's Close contains the Roman Eagle Hall, with a plaster ceiling dated 1646.

17 LOTHIAN REGION OFFICES,
George IV Bridge
Robert Matthew Johnson-Marshall and Partners, 1970.

Offices, canteens etc. for Lothian Region, linked by tunnel under George IV Bridge to the old Midlothian County Buildings by McIntyre Henry 1900-05. Although modulated when observed uphill from Victoria Street, its horizontality and large scale of detail sits uneasily with its neighbours, and suffers by external comparison with the florid Edwardian baroque of the older building across the road.

18 435 LAWNMARKET
Late 17th century.

Tall plain, rubble built land, with wallhead gable, reasonable stone dressings to windows, and restored Victoriana on the ground two floors.

The Crown of St. Giles

Bank of Scotland

19 BANK OF SCOTLAND, The Mound
Robert Reid and Richard Crichton,
1802-06.

Originally a sedate classical building perched
high on the edge of the Old Town; later
floridly extended in Roman Baroque, with
some French touches, and a protruding dome
with a Cyclops eye, by David Bryce, 1865-70;
pavilioned terrace rebuilt by Peddie &
Kinnear, 1878. Impressive stairhall; banking
hall now horizontally divided.

20 HIGH KIRK OF ST. GILES, High Street

Formerly the only parish church within the
city walls, briefly translated to Cathedral
status on the orders of Charles I in 1633. The
Choir, with mediaeval vault and eastern bay
added about 1460, is wholly original, but only
the crowned tower, dating from 1500 and
restored in the 17th century, escaped the
necessary refacing by William Burn in 1829.
Interior restored as single church and main
arcades on nave rebuilt by William Hay, an
ex-assistant of G. G. Scott in 1870-83; his
also is the west door with sculpture by the
Rhinds. The latest addition is the Chapel of
the most Ancient and most Noble Order of
the Thistle by Sir Robert Lorimer in 1910
containing splendid craftsmanship of stone,
timber and glass. General repairs and
basement extension begun 1981, by Bernard
Feilden, Simpson and Brown.
Guide book available.

St. Giles

Parliament Square, original drawing by Robert Reid

Parliament House of Scotland **above:** original east face, by Gordon of Rothiemay 1647 **Below:** surviving interior, drawn by R W Billings, 1846

21 PARLIAMENT HALL and HIGH COURT OF JUSTICIARY
1632-9.

Built as a free standing, L-shaped Parliament building with two halls, one above the other, which, with its square, was a key building in the Scots architectural renaissance of the 16th/17th centuries, of which a number of other significant buildings remain in Edinburgh; and which deserves more detailed notice than it has received so far (the neglect probably resulting from the historic but ill-founded view that Scots architecture of this period is a dim copy of early building in England). Lord Cockburn detested the classical refacing: *no one who remembers the old exterior can see the new one without sorrow and indignation. . . The old building exhibited some respectable turrets, some ornamental windows and doors and a handsome balustrade.* The Parliament Square facade which thus earned his displeasure, with rusticated arcade and prominent Ionic pedimented centrepiece, is by Robert Reid, 1807-10 and 1825-34. Only a small portion of the original exterior remains; a portion of the west facade visible from George IV Bridge.
Parliament Hall is 122 feet long, and has the original 49 foot wide hammerbeam roof, constructed by John Scott c. 1640. The illustration shows the hall in 1846, since when further alterations have taken place. **Laigh Hall** beneath, retains its arcade of octagonal stone piers, and the original fireplace. Prior to the construction of the Advocate's Library, the books were held herein: prior to that, horses' stabling. Interesting series of unaltered courtrooms by Archibald Elliot (1818, remodelled by William Nixon 1849), Robert Reid (1825-34), W. W. Robertson (1885) and W. T. Oldrieve (1908).

Signet Library

SIGNET LIBRARY, Parliament Square Interior by **William Stark,** 1813, completed by **Robert Reid.**

Two libraries, one above the other, linked by grand triumphal staircase by William Playfair, 1819, and reconstructed in 1833 by William Burn. The Upper Library is a classical cathedral: 136 feet long, bays defined by Corinthian columns, vaulted with a semi-eliptical coffered ceiling. The crossing has massed Corinthian pilasters, and a shallow, rooflit dome painted by Thomas Stothard: the triforium is represented by a continuous upper balcony with fine ironwork.

CHARLES II STATUE, Parliament Square Cast in lead 1685.

The only extant equestrian statue of the monarch in Great Britain.

MERCAT CROSS, Parliament Square

Capital originally 15th century, but shaft a 1970 copy of parts of the 15th century shaft salvaged when the original (which was about half as tall again) was shattered in 1756, on the grounds that it impeded traffic. A local poet concluded, conversely, that its demolition was because Bonnie Prince Charlie had proclaimed his father's right to the throne thereon. Octagonal cross-house, 1885, a copy by Sydney Mitchell of the original (demolished in 1756) based on old drawings and engravings.

22 BYER'S CLOSE, 373 High Street 17 century.

A tall, thin house distinguished by its three sided apse capped by carved, heraldic pedimented windows facing north. Named after Bishop Adam Bothwell of Orkney. Built as something of a garden pavilion looking out

to the view over the Forth. Now hemmed in, requiring attention, and best seen from Advocate's Close. The truncated 17th century rubble built street facade retains a certain grim grandeur.
The Closes off the High Street have all been treated to improvement works supervised by Robert Hurd and Partners. One forgets what they used to be like. Here is Dorothy Wordsworth in 1822: *What horrible alleys on each side of the High Street, especially downwards like passes of quarries of dark stone. I ventured down one, and hastened back to escape from the spitting of two children who were leaning out of an upper window...* In 1819 Robert Southey had been more terse: *The Wyndes, down which an English eye may look but into which no English nose would willingly venture-for stinks older then the Union are to be found there.''*

Adam Bothwell's House, Byers Close

The City Chambers, the engraved frontispiece to the original building contract for building the City Chambers, by J Fergus 1754

23 *CITY CHAMBERS,* 249 High Street
1753-61

Built as the Royal Exchange by John Fergus adapting a design by John Adam. Courtyard development, open to the street through a single-storey, rusticated screen. Central block weakly pedimented and pilastered: much more powerful in the drawing than in the execution. As an Exchange, the building was a failure; Smollett, commenting through **Humphrey Clinker** in 1766 noted *All the people of business at Edinburgh, and even the genteel company, may be seen standing in crowds everyday from one to two in the afternoon . . . at a place where formerly stood a market cross. . . The people stand in the open from force of custom, rather than move a few yards to an Exchange that stands empty on one side.* Altered and adapted for City Council use, the northern, boldly Baroque wing facing Cockburn Street by Robert Morham (1890 and 1900) contains the Council Chamber. Historic Mary King's Close survives underneath the western flank. The north part of the original building, eleven storeys high is one of the tallest buildings remaining in the Old Town. (But it may not have been the tallest: a fourteen storey tenement was observed in the 18th century, at the back of Parliament Square, leading down to the Cowgate.)

24 EDINBURGH WAX MUSEUM,
New Assembly Close
Gillespie Graham, 1813.

Built as Commercial Bank. Rather
provincial mid-Georgian, three bay,
centrepiece triumphal arch in giant engaged
order. Fine ironwork. Converted to the Wax
Museum by John C. Hope.

25 TRON KIRK, High Street
John Mylne, founded in 1633.

Originally T-Plan but shortened and shorn
of its south aisle on construction of South
Bridge by John Baxter 1785-87. Current
steeple by R. & R. Dickson 1829, much
larger and more formal than the one it
replaced. Kirk exterior restored by Andrew
Renton 1973, but interior gutted, revealing
causeway, and foundations of Marlin's
Wynd over which it was built. A fine
hammerbeam roof survives, enriched with
guilt knops, comparable to and
contemporary with that in the Parliament
Hall. Late Gothic window tracery and
panelled clasping buttresses of considerable
interest. It was in this Kirk, in 1693, that a
Mr Areskine is reported as praying *Lord,
have mercy on a' fool and idiots, and
particularly on the Magistrates of
Edinburgh.*
Lord Cockburn watched original steeple
being destroyed by fire in 1824: *an old
Dutch thing composed of wood and iron and
lead edged all the way up with bits of
ornament. . . There could not be a more
beautiful firework. . . The fire seized on
every projecting point, and played with the
fretwork as if it had been all an exhibition.*
It was similar only to four other known
examples: St. Ninian's Manse, Leith (p. 78)
which survives yet; the north west tower of
Holyrood abbey; the main steeple of the
original 17th century Glasgow University,
and that of Dumfries Town Hall (modelled
on Glasgow). The steeple of the Well Court
Hall, Dean Village, is a scaled-down version
of the Tron original. When the church spire
had to be substantially repaired in the 1970s,
a move was made to rebuild the original;
talked out by Sir Robert Matthew who
considered that the existing one made a
greater contribution to Edinburgh's skyline.

26 199 HIGH STREET
Early 18th century.

Fine seven storey tenement with wallhead
gable on the corner of Cockburn Street.
Recently renovated by the City Architects'
Department to its former grandeur.

27 COCKBURN STREET
Peddie and Kinnear, 1860.

Curved, sloping, cobbled street in variegated
Scots Baronial which cut across original
closes and tenements, leading down to the
Nor' Loch.

RCAHMS

Tron Kirk **Above:** *north front in 1753, engraved by
William Whitlend.* **Below:** *the east front today*

28 CITY ART GALLERY, Market Street
Dunn and Findlay, 1899.

A baroque warehouse of some quality, with
ordered rows of arched windows, converted
by Edinburgh District Council Architects,
1980, into the new City Art Gallery. First
floor cut back to provide grand double height
entrance hall. Excellent, fin-de-siècle, mural-
covered café.

29 NORTH BRIDGE
Dunn and Findlay 1899-1902 (west side),
W. Hamilton and A. R. Scott and Sydney
Mitchell 1898 (east side).

As one looks south from the North Bridge,
the Scotsman building and Carlton Hotel
form one of Edinburgh's finest gateways; the
romantic turrets signifying the transition
between the classical New Town and the
exotic old one. The North Bridge itself was
rebuilt 1896-97 by Cunningham Blyth &
Westland with architecture by Robert
Morham.

City Art Gallery

30 LAURIE MEMORIAL HALL, Jeffrey Street
Shaw-Stewart, Blaikie & Perry, 1962.

Attached to William Hay and George
Henderson's Old St. Paul's Episcopal Church
of 1883; notable interior of Gerona type with
a magnificent reredos.

31 HOLY TRINITY CHURCH HALL,
Chalmers Close
15th century, re-erected late 19th century.

Sad rump of one of Scotland's finest
mediaeval buildings, constructed from the
Choir of Trinity College Church which was
demolished for railway sidings at Waverley.
All stones were numbered to permit re-
erection elsewhere, but were pilfered for
building materials and garden ornaments
during disagreements over what should be
done. *An outrage by sordid traders* fulminated
Lord Cockburn, *virtually consented to by a
tasteless city and sanctioned by an insensible
Parliament. . . These people would remove Pompeii
for a railway and tell us they had applied it to better
purpose in Dundee.* Sir Patrick Geddes added:
*this railway system has not been the utilitarian
success it still pretends itself, but has been not merely
half-ruinous to the beauty of Edinburgh, but
structurally bungled and economically wasteful to all
concerned.*
Trinity Church hall is all that remains,
principally constructed from the choir and
apse. Individual stones, niches and corbels of
the highest quality may be perceived built
into the walls. The illustration by Billings
shows the Church just prior to demolition and
may have been drawn specifically at the
request of David Bryce who originally secured
the task of reconstruction. Those charming
their way inside will find that it is a very
beautiful fragment.

*Trinity College Church, engraved by R W Billings just
prior to dismantling.* **Above:** *exterior from the west*
Below: *interior of the choir*

32 MOUBRAY HOUSE, 53 High Street
16th century, on a 15th century base.

Four storey town house, with curved
forestair, which extends over four times its
street frontage behind. Clearly of some
original quality, to judge by the quality of
masonry and string courses. The projecting
timber gable is plastered. Fine plaster ceiling
inside.

33 JOHN KNOX'S HOUSE, 45 High Street
16th century composite structure around
earlier nucleus.

The most conspicuous building in the Old
Town projecting into the High Street.
Architecturally curious, having two separate
staircases giving access to different parts.
Interesting fusion of a quality stone building
of good masonry, window details, inscribed
pancls and roundels, and the more
picturesque timber projections, galleries and
gables (mostly modern renewals). The initials
"JM" are those of James Mossman,
goldsmith to Mary Queen of Scots. Pantiled
roof and recasting of the interior is by Robert
Hurd and Partners, who uncovered
previously unknown painted panels.

As Brereton noted above, many High Street
buildings sported timber frontages. The
reason was as follows: in 1508 the King
permitted Edinburgh citizens to let the
Common lands of the Borough Muir, who
promptly cleared the land of its timber. As
recorded by the 18th century historian
Maitland'; *to encourage the inhabitants to purchase
the said wood, the Town Council enacted that
whoever should buy a quantity thereof sufficient to
new front the Tenement he, she, or they dwelt in,
should be allowed to extend the said new front, the
space of seven feet into the street; whereby the High
Street was reduced fourteen feet in its breadth; and the
buildings which before had stonern fronts were now
converted into wood, and the Burgh into a wooden
City.* In 1598, Fynes Moryson recorded *The
outsides are faced with wooden galleries built upon
the second storey of the houses: yet these galleries give
the owners a fair and pleasant prospect.* They also
gave the occupants, the only opportunity of
taking the air without encountering the often
revolting condition of the pavements.

34 TWEEDDALE HOUSE, 14 High Street
1576.

Additions late 17th century by Sir William
Bruce, reconstructed mid 18th century, with a
further addition 1791. In 1724 Daniel Defoe
noted *The Marquess of Tweedale has a good City
House, with a plantation of lime-trees behind it
instead of a garden.* Subsequently it became a
Bank and then a Publishing House. Currently
under restoration by Roland Wedgewood and
Partners, again as a publishing house.

Shona Adam

John Knox's House

McKean

Moray House

Chessels Court

35 CHESSEL'S COURT, 240 Canongate
About 1748.

Early mansion flats. The south building is of great quality, and some of its flats have rococo chimney-pieces and other original details. Restored by Robert Hurd & Partners 1964, with new buildings completing the courtyard on east and north sides.

36 186-198 CANONGATE
17th century.

Three storey building with symmetrical dormered front, with a turnpike stair tower in Old Playhouse Close, the wing on the west side having a semi-octagonal stair tower. Much rebuilt in 1968-69 by Gordon and Dey as part of the Moray House complex. Behind is the Masonic Lodge, Canongate Kilwinning, 17th century and 1735-36, still retaining much of its original atmosphere and said to be oldest Lodge room extant anywhere in the world.

In no. 190 Tobias Smollett spent some months with his sister in 1766. The following extract from **Humphrey Clinker** is the result of that visit. *The first thing that strikes the nose of a stranger shall be nameless; but what first strikes the eye is the unconscionable height of the houses. . . This manner of building, attended with numberless inconveniences, must have been originally owing to want of room . . . Today . . . we are settled in convenient lodgings, up four pairs of stairs in the High Street, the fourth storey being, in this city, reckoned more genteel than the first. Every storey is a compleat house, occupied by a separate family; and the stair being common to them all is generally left in a very filthy condition: a man must tread with great circumspection to get safe housed with unpolluted shoes.*

37 MORAY HOUSE, 174 Canongate
c. 1628.

Perhaps the finest aristocratic mansion to survive in the Old Town, Moray House was built by Mary, Dowager Countess of Home. Defoe regarded both Moray House and Queensberry House as *very magnificent, large and princely buildings, all of Free stone, large in front, with good gardens behind them.* Yet in 1723, the perceptive J. Macky had noted of the Canongate *the prime nobility built their palaces here, and those that were obliged to attend the Court took Lodgings here; so that nothing can be supposed to have suffered so much by the Union as this street.* That forecast of decline was prophetic. Moray House is L-shaped, with a two-storeyed street-front, a balcony corbelled from the first-floor of the gable wing, which has a semi-octagonal stair tower on the side, (visible behind the notable pyramid-capped gate piers.) That wing contains fine Renaissance plaster ceilings. The building is now part of Moray House College of Education, the nucleus of which is a heavy Renaissance quadrangle fronting Holyrood Road by Alan K. Robertson, 1913. The famous garden pavilion, in which the Treaty of Union between England and Scotland was signed by the "parcel of rogues" is relegated to standing pantiled and isolated in a dark vehicle service access.

Canongate Tolbooth

Huntly House

38 TOLBOOTH, 163 Canongate
1592.

Canongate was formerly a separate burgh,
and the Tolbooth its civic centre. The Council
Chamber, on the first floor, is reached by an
outside stair. The powerful turreted steeple is
characteristic of Scottish Tolbooths although
less fortified than some, and shows French
Château influence. Restored in 1879 by
Robert Morham, who added the dormered
wallhead. Note adjacent early 17th century
house with turnpike stair at nos. 167-9.

39 HUNTLY HOUSE, 146 Canongate
1570.

Gabled building, the top two storeys of which
are of white-plastered timber construction
jettied out over the two lower storeys of stone.
The upper storey clearly the principal floor,
with dressed stone, regular windows and
string course. Ground floor has rough rubble
and small windows. It is now a City Museum
and contains relics from other demolished
buildings. Originally nicknamed the *Speaking
House* from the collection of didactic stone
mottos built into the facade for the edification
of passers-by.
Restored by Sir Frank Mears in 1924; and
no. 142 restored by Ian G. Lindsay and
Partners 1968-9. **Bakehouse Close** to the rear
forms with Acheson House (see below) one of
the best preserved closes in the Royal Mile.

Bakehouse Close, drawn in 1885 by Ernest George

Acheson House, just after restoration in 1937

Canongate Church

40 ACHESON HOUSE, 146 Canongate
1633-34.

Three storey hôtel, now entered through the side, though retaining its own small walled front forecourt on to Bakehouse Close. Initials SAA and SMH are for Sir Archibald Acheson and his wife, Dame Margaret Hamilton. Restored in 1937 for the Marquis of Bute by Robert Hurd, and now the Scottish Craft Centre.

41 CANONGATE CHURCH and CHURCHYARD
James Smith, 1688.

Designed for the Congregation which was displaced by King James VII when he converted the Abbey Church at Holyroodhouse into a Chapel for the Knights of the Thistle. Plain, cruciform, aisled church, with decoratively gabled south front topped by antlers, and pierced by a diminutive Doric portico. Many interesting memorials in the churchyard, from which fine views of Calton Hill may be obtained.

42 PANMURE HOUSE,
off Little Lochend Close
17th century.

A plain little house of the lesser gentry: L-plan rubble mansion with crow-stepped gables, and raised courtyard. Adam Smith, Economist and author of *The Wealth of Nations* lived here 1778-90.

43 3, 5, and 6 REID'S COURT
Early 18th century.

Two storey, white harled, main block with wings, built as a pleasant country mansion: note ornate, scrolled skews. Restored in 1958 by Ian G. Lindsay & Partners, as a manse for the Canongate Church.

44 79-121 CANONGATE
Sir Basil Spence Glover and Ferguson, 1966-8.

Vigorous development of three four-storey blocks of flats, comprising some of the most stimulating modern architecture in Edinburgh, particularly the geometry of the balconies at the rear.

45 82 CANONGATE
City Architects' Department, 1954

Post-war reconstruction of 1619 Nisbet of
Dirleton's house, with its crow-stepped gables
and stair tower, incorporating some of the
original stones and carved lintels. Perhaps a
few centuries of weathering will restore its
antique flavour. Nisbet of Dirleton was a
celebrated anti-Covenanter Judge of the
Court of Session, whose reputation was such
as (allegedly) to earn the following comment
from the Lord Clerk Register: *Thow rotten old
devil, thow wilt get thyself stabbed some day.* The
prophesy proved inaccurate.

46 QUEENSBERRY HOUSE, 64 Canongate
James Smith, 1682.

Large, altered and heightened mansion, its
former quality clearly testified by Defoe's
opinion (see Moray House, above); later
remodelled as barracks 1808. Contemporary
with Smith's greater house for the same
client, Drumlanrig Castle, though now
showing little trace of the connection. Many
internal details removed to Gosford House,
East Lothian.

47 WHITE HORSE CLOSE, 31 Canongate
17th century.

The former White Horse Inn, restored by
J. Jerdan, 1889, and by Sir Frank Mears and
Partners, 1964. Now a group of 15 homes
around a courtyard entered from the
Canongate through a pend under a wholly

Whitehorse Close

new front block with peculiar arcading. Once
inside, an assembly of picturesque elements:
crow step gables, jettied bays, dormer
windows, and elegant external staircases.

48 11-15 CANONGATE
1697.

Four storey tenement capped by three crow-
stepped gables facing the street. Restored by
Robert Hurd & Partners, 1976, with thick
white harling.

*The Canongate from the Holyrood Port, drawn by Paul
Sandby in 1749. The Abbey gateway was demolished soon
afterwards. 11-15 Canongate can be seen behind*

Edinburgh District Council

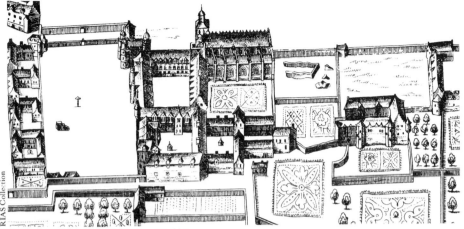

Holyrood Precincts in 1647, by Gordon of Rothiemay

49 HOLYROOD and its PRECINCTS

The Abbey of Holyrood was one of Scotland's richest ecclesiastical foundations. In the later part of the 15th century, the Abbot's Guest House became used by the Kings of Scotland as their Edinburgh residence in preference to the draughty castle. In the 16th century, the Kings began to develop a Royal Palace here, the Abbey becoming the Chapel Royal.

Fountain, drawn by Jessie King, 1906

FOUNTAIN, Palace Yard

Constructed in 1859 to designs by Robert Matheson: the figures designed by his clerk Charles Doyle, brother of Dicky and father of Arthur Conan. Modelled on fountain at Linlithgow Palace.

ABBEY STRAND (WEST)
16th century.

Four storeyed mansion, top storey later, recast in present form by Thomas Ross 1915.

ABBEY STRAND (EAST)
17th century.

Known as Lucky Spence's house, this is a two storey old fashioned building with three crow-stepped gables facing street. Modern arched pend leading to shop.

ABBEY COURT HOUSE, Palace Yard
16th century and later.

Oblong rubble building with circular tower on gable with fine ogee door-head. Wall to Abbey Strand shows traces of original Abbey pend arcading. Superb Renaisance doorway just to south, rebuilt from the pre-Bruce palace; thought to have been the doorway from palace to garden. The drawing by Paul Sandby (1749) is of the view west, through the vaulted pend, to the Canongate, with 11-15 Canongate in the centre.

PALACE OF HOLYROODHOUSE

The north west tower, 16th century, is all that survives of the pre-Civil War palace. In 1661. J. de Rocheford described how the old palace consisted of the *first great court, composed of several small pavilions intermixed with galleries and turrets, forming a wonderful symmetry. There is also likewise the church, the cloisters and the gardens of this ancient abbey.* The remainder is late 17th century to the design of Sir William Bruce, executed by Robert Mylne, the King's Master Mason. Bruce balanced the old tower with one on the north east, forming a grand, arcaded quadrangle between, the two towers tied by a rusticated screen wall. He also balanced the Abbey ruins on the north with a mock ecclesiastical kitchen wing on the south, subsequently demolished.

Holyrood Palace, from Maitland's **History of Edinburgh**

The contract to rebuild the Palace survives in full detail and is of great interest. Dated March 1672, it is between Sir William Bruce (His Majesty's Surveyor General), Sir William Sharp (His Majesty's Cash Keeper) and Robert Mylne (His Majesty's Master Mason). **Inter-alia,** it specified: *ITEM: to build the whole walls round the said Court. . . in exact, fine ashlar work . . . with three entablatures round the said Court within and without: the first at the first floor of the Dorricke Order: the second at the second floor of the Ionicke Order: And the third round the top of the walls within and without of the Corinthian Order. All of them having their true proportions, ornaments and projections of fine well cut and joined stone work.*

ABBEY OF HOLYROODHOUSE
Founded by **David I** in 1128.

Ruined early 13th century nave and west front, (altered 1633) are the sole remains of this magnificent building. The south aisle is still vaulted, and there is fine blind arcading. The nave was converted to the Chapel Royal in 17th century and then again to Chapel of the Order of the Thistle. The west front was closed, with sole access through the palace. Much work then carried out, including curious traceried windows in both east and west ends, (surviving) and a new hat for the north western tower like the Tron Kirk steeple; the disastrous roofing in stone slates —which caused the building's destruction in the following century, was added in 1758. In 1829 Felix Mendelssohn visited the Abbey at twilight: *Everything is in ruins and mouldering, and the bright light of heaven shines in. I believe I have found the beginning of my Scottish Symphony there today.* **Guide book available.**

RCAHMS

The inside of Holyrood Abbey after conversion into the Chapel Royal, from **Vitruvius Scoticus**

*Holyrood Abbey ruins.
Compare to the drawing
of the Chapel Royal*

*Queen Mary's
Bath House,
drawn by Jessie King,
1906*

Croft an Righ

SUNDIAL, North Garden
John Mylne, 1633.

Octagonal pedestal with polyhedron head.

50 QUEEN MARY'S BATH HOUSE, Abbeyhill
Late 16th century.

Two storey, rubble building (possibly built as a pavilion.) The drawing by Jessie M. King, 1906, lends it a willowy slenderness that eludes it in reality.

51 CROFT AN RIGH
16th century.

Small L-shaped country mansion tucked away behind the Palace, of three and four storeys, with conical roofed turrets on south side, and fine interior plasterwork.

COWGATE

One of the oldest thoroughfares in Edinburgh. In 1550 it was described as *where the nobility and chief men of the city reside, and in which are the palaces of the officers of State.* Later commentators refer to it as a *great street.* Although Robert Forsyth, in 1805, attributed its decline to *falling into decay in consequence of the extension of the city into more favourable situations,* the greatest damage to the Cowgate was inflicted by the construction of the South and George IV bridges, which effectively relegated the Cowgate to *below stairs.* By 1840 it had become *the most densely peopled and poorest district in the metropolis, —altogether squalid in its appearance. Seen from George IV's bridge, it looks like a dark narrow river of architecture moving sluggishly along a dell and teeming with animated being . . . were it raised out of its ravine hiding place . . . it would be an utter blot and defilement on the whole picture of the metropolis.* Since that time the Cowgate, along with the Pleasance, has been largely cleared, and left substantially desolate. Some items remain, and the future seems more promising.

RCAHMS

McKean

Medieval landscape with Tardis. The Flodden Wall at the south-east corner of the City, where it descends to the Cowgate. 33 St. Mary Street can be seen in the distance. The building whose roof appears above the wall is the old Surgeon's Hall

52 POLLOCK INSTITUTE, Pleasance
J. Inch Morrison, 1925-37.

Appealing group of pantiled buildings created out of a former brewery and grouped with the Quaker Meeting House of 1791.

53 FLODDEN WALL,
corner Pleasance/Drummond Street.

Edinburgh was a fortified city, the last of whose gates—the Netherbow—survived to mid 18th century. Only significant surviving remains are of the Flodden Wall, built in early 16th century, allegedly consequent upon the battle of Flodden, but still incomplete fifty years afterwards—in spite of a capital levy per head of the population. Surviving portions indicate a rubble wall about 25 feet high, with few features: a good stretch of wall can be viewed at the corner of Pleasance/Drummond Street; the best preserved tower is at the Vennel, West Port, above the Grassmarket.

54 OLD SURGEON'S HALL,
High School Yards
James Smith, 1696-97.

Originally, a curvilinear fronted, flamboyant three-storey building set low in the last surviving corner of the Flodden Wall, with projecting stair towers; later rendered much plainer by alterations. Its northern facade retains an austere elegance. In 1703, the Hall was described as a *very pretty bagnio and a hall . . . newly built . . . here is somewhat of a collection of anatomys.* One house of the former Surgeon's Square to the north of it survives.

55 OLD HIGH SCHOOL, Infirmary Street
Alexander Laing, 1777.

Plain two storey building with Doric portico. *Oblong structure of tawny stone* wrote George Borrow *with many windows fenced in with wire*

netting, with thy long hall below, and thy five chambers above, for the reception of the five classes, into which the eight-hundred urchins, who styled thee instructress, were divided. Reconstructed with tower Sir R. Rowand Anderson 1905-7, and now used as geographical department, University of Edinburgh.

56 33 ST. MARY'S STREET
Moira, Moira, Wann, 1977.

A pity the planners required this new building to be set back: it is one of the ancient gateways to Edinburgh whose sense of enclosure has now been lost. That said, this corner office development adopts old forms and patterns with some sensitivity. More could have been made (with fewer materials) of the corner.

57 ST. PATRICK'S CHURCH,
South Grays Close (facing Cowgate)
1771.

Consecrated as an Episcopal Church, but now Roman Catholic. Interior re-orientated, 1898. Slender tower with octagonal chamber and lead covered dome. Heavy new front and terrace by Reginald Fairlie, 1928-29.

St. Patrick's Church

Scott Robertson

East Side of Blackfriars Street, drawing by Edinburgh District Council. 4 New Skinners Close can be seen in the centre and 51-55 Blackfriars Street on the right

58 BLACKFRIARS STREET

Formerly Blackfriar's Wynd; eastern side rebuilt in 1870-73, mainly by David Clunas under the City Improvement Act. The church is by Robert Morham. The City of Edinburgh is now part way through a substantial programme of rehabilitation and infill. Blackfriars Wynd was one of the key thoroughfares in the Old Town containing a significant number of grand mansions, including the now demolished Cardinal Beaton's Palace on the Cowgate corner.

4 NEW SKINNERS CLOSE
(off 31 Blackfriars Street)
Early 18th century.

L-plan building with large semi-octagonal stair tower in re-entrant, and moulded doorway. Part possibly earlier. Originally, Cross House, and probably rebuilt in present form as the Skinner's Hall. In 1857 Dr. Thomas Guthrie founded his "Ragged School" here. Now restored as housing by the City Architects' Department (1982).

REGENT MORTON'S HOUSE,
8 Blackfriar's Street
Late 16th Century.

Much altered but still restoreable survival of a nobleman's mansion. Later windows, and alterations to wall surface are a legacy from the fact that under 100 years ago this house had a fine, projecting, timber gallery. Finest surviving part of the Regent's house is projecting semi-octagonal staircase with ogival doorhead and carved tympanum, of a type once common in Edinburgh.

TENEMENT, 51-55 Blackfriars Street
Edinburgh District Council Architects,
1981.

Distinctive, modern block of flats enhanced by ziggurat details in post-modern style, somewhat let down by treatment of ground floor. Designed to harmonise with 17th century style City Improvement Trust tenements.

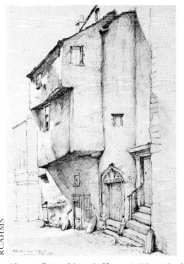

RCAHMS

Above: *Regent Morton's House. A lithograph after James Drummond 1879. The projecting timber galleries no longer exist, but could be replaced. As an aristocrat's house, the building is of a different type and just as significant as Gladstone's Land* **Below:** *51-55 Blackfriars Street*

Scott Robertson

C

St Cecilia's Hall

Tailor's Hall

59 ST. CECILIA'S HALL, Niddry Street
(facing Cowgate)
Robert Mylne, 1763.

Unprepossessing exterior, but interior a gem;
oval concert hall, staircase and Laigh Hall,
restored and extended 1966 for Edinburgh
University by Ian G. Lindsay & Partners, to
house the Russell Collection of early
keyboard instruments.

60 10-20 ROBERTSON CLOSE
17th century.

Restoration of early tenements to provide 11
flats by Nicholas Groves-Raines: harled,
octagonal, turreted projected staircase, and
fine stone dressings.

61 SOUTH BRIDGE
Alexander Laing, 1786.

A viaduct of 19 arches, only one of
which—over the Cowgate—is now
perceptible, linking the High Street to the
South Side. Lined by dull buildings by
Robert Kay, of a few years later. Their best
feature are the pedimented gables seen from
the Cowgate.

62 TAILOR'S HALL, Cowgate
Possibly complete by 1621.

Corporate seat of the Incorporation of
Tailors. Formed south side of enclosed square
with projecting staircase to east. Had one of
the finest street frontages in old Edinburgh—
now demolished. Grossly altered when a
brewery, but retains original details: e.g. fine
door and window lintels. Impressive, and
restoreable.

63 SOLICITORS' BUILDINGS, Cowgate
James Bow Dunn, 1889.

Library Hall above, linked to the Court of
Session, in fantastic red sandstone Gothic,
with oriels and gargoyles; tenement flats
below on to Cowgate, neglected.

Solicitor's Buildings

Magdalen Chapel, drawing by Hanslip Fletcher 1910

64 MAGDALEN CHAPEL, 30 Cowgate
Founded in 1541, tower built in 1621, street
frontage indifferent late Victorian.

The stained glass is the only Scottish pre-
Reformation example surviving in its original
building. Interior contains Jacobean-style
arcaded timber panelling, good ironwork and
plain barrel-vaulted plaster ceiling.
Renovation work started by George Hay in
1960.

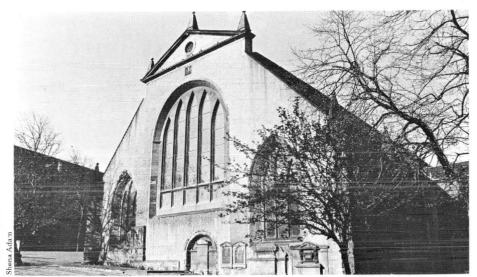

Shena Adam

Greyfriar's Church

65 36 CANDLEMAKER ROW
1722.

Four-storey, rubble Guildhall of Corporation of Candlemakers, adjacent to earlier tenements. Two square, projecting stair towers (one gabled with armorial pancl) and moulded doorway. Nos. 46 and 52, restored for Cockburn Preservation Trust 1980 by Simpson and Brown.

66 GREYFRIARS CHURCH
and CHURCHYARD, Candlemaker Row
Eastern Part 1620

Church with aisles, buttresses and Gothic windows, perhaps derived from the former Friary which existed nearby, and possibly incorporating pieces of the demolished convent of St. Catherine of Sienna; highly anachronistic for 1620. East gable capped by simple, pinnacled pediment. Another church was added to the west end, replacing a tower, by Alexander McGill in 1722. The whole was formed into a unified church after restoration works in 1938 by Henry Kerr. The Churchyard, in which the National Covenant was signed in 1638, is of awesome monumental grandeur. It includes the burial place of the Adam family of architects, with the fine mausoleum by John and Robert; now in disrepair. **Guide book available.**

67 AUGUSTINE BRISTO
CONGREGATIONAL CHURCH,
George IV Bridge
J., J. M. & W. H. Hay, Liverpool, 1857-61.

Free Romanesque, with a wedding-cake steeple.

Simpson and Brown

52 Candlemaker Row, seen from Greyfriar's Church Yard

68 PUBLIC LIBRARY, George IV Bridge
George Washington Browne, 1887.

Finest of his Fancois Ier-style buildings in the Capital. Annexe and bank on corner of Victoria Street elegant neo-Jacobean by John Henderson 1836-37, with sculpture group by A. H. Ritchie.

69 VICTORIA STREET
Planned by **Thomas Hamilton,** 1827, revised by **George Smith,** 1840
North side built 1840-46.

Arcaded shopfronts carrying a pedestrian terrace above and forming a base for a scenic architectural background comprising former Mechanics Hall (rear of Riddle's Court) by George Smith, flanked by two Italian Gothic churches by Paterson and Shiells, 1865. The finest individual building is India Buildings, David Cousin 1864, business chambers with a domed and galleried circular concourse in the middle.

Thompson's Court proposal

Part of the elevation of 93-101 West Bow, drawn by Thomas Hamilton prior to his reconstruction of the upper part. This section survives

70 89, 93-101 WEST BOW, 108-110 GRASSMARKET

The foot of the present Victoria Street is the lower end of the original West Bow, which survived the 1829 improvements. There are still extant five of the old houses, comprising 89 West Bow, 91-93 West Bow, 95-99 West Bow, 102 West Bow and the corner house between West Bow and Grassmarket known as No. 1 Grassmarket. They are all four or five storeys in height and of late 17th century or early 18th century date and present a fine array of gables: crow-stepped, wallhead, and curvilinear with bulls-eyes. Interior of No. 91 is complete and virtually unaltered.

71 GRASSMARKET

Edinburgh's most atmospheric urban space, a 230 yard long rectangle under the lee of the castle cliff. Site of former market and executions. Buildings of various ages, mostly now later Victorian.

72 THOMSON'S COURT, CASTLE WYND, Grassmarket
Proposed development by **Michael Calthrop and Campbell Mars.**

Sheltered housing scheme of 30 flats for Edinvar Housing Association to fill a notorious gap in north side of Grassmarket. Scheme owes much to symbolism to Ramsay Gardens, high on the hill above.

Portsburgh Square

73 CASTLECLIFF WORKSHOPS, Johnston Terrace
Royal Engineers, 1872.

Originally a plain barrack block for army married quarters, towers added in 1874 by City Architect Robert Morham, in deference to the city's objection to its severe appearance. Restored as workshops 1977-80 by J. R. Marshall and H. de Burgh.

74 PORTSBURGH SQUARE, West Port
City Architect's Department, 1900.

Workman's tenement flats in three sides of a Baronial square, restored to beauty by T. M. Gray and Associates.

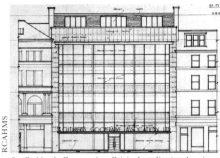

St. Cuthbert's Co-operative. Original application drawing

75 ST. CUTHBERT'S CO OPERATIVE,
Bread Street
T. Waller Marwick, 1937.

The first sheer, glazed, curtain-walled building in Edinburgh whose purity is degraded by being painted in pastel colours. The same architect was earlier responsible for the scenic domed corner building at the Fountainbridge gusset in association with his father T. Purves Marwick, 1914.

76 KING'S BRIDGE, Johnston Terrace
Thomas Hamilton, 1827.

Flyover bridge with four obelisks carrying the new Johnston Terrace over King's Stables Road: best viewed from King's Stables Road.

77 CASTLE TERRACE and SPITTAL STREET
Sir James Gowans, 1868-70.

Super-tenement of original detail and striking silhouette, designed upon Gowans' geometrical principles, the proportions being multiples of 2 with 45° angle on face plan and 67½° on elevation. Gowans' design method was an early example of modular proportion: with all items in multiples of 2 feet, he was able to standardise windows, doors and furniture. After training in Bryce's office, he had turned to railway engineering, thence to improved housing for working-class people. He became the largest lessee of quarries in Scotland, his houses in Napier road with their different coloured stones (p. 99) an advertisement of that fact. His interests included tramways, theatres, Building Standards and the 1886 Edinburgh International Exhibition for which he was knighted.

78 ST. MARK'S UNITARIAN CHURCH,
Castle Terrace
David Bryce, 1834.

Handsome composition of grand, South German Baroque windows, with a vertical strength that dominates the horizontal, curving late Georgian Terrace.

Castle Terrace

79 ST. CUTHBERTS CHURCH
and CHURCHYARD, Lothian Road

The steeple of 1789 by Alexander Stevens was the only part of the plain 18th century *God Box* retained in the design of the present church, 1894, by Hippolyte J. Blanc. The Georgian church had in fact replaced a ruinous church of much greater antiquity. The sobriety of the new one attracted great unpopularity *a great barn, totally unsuitable to the situation in which it is placed* etc. Spectacular Renaissance apse with sculpture by Bridgman and murals by Sir Gerald Moira, one window by Tiffany. War Memorial chapel designed by P. MacGregor Chalmers.

80 SCOTTISH FILM COUNCIL, Lothian Road
David Bryce, 1830.

Former Lothian Road Burgher Meeting House now converted into a film centre by the Waters Jamieson Partnership. Twin projecting pavilions, in standard Georgian residential vocabulary. One of Bryce's earliest commissions, carried out from his house.

Usher Hall, as first built

Lauriston Place

81 USHER HALL, Lothian Road
Stockdale Harrison, 1910.

Octagonal, domed expression of industry's support for the arts, in railway station Baroque of E. A. Rickards' type. Symmetrical disposition of facades belies plan set askew on difficult site. Equally grandiose interior.

82 ROYAL LYCEUM THEATRE,
Grindlay Street
C. J. Phipps, 1883.

Late Victorian interior gaudily restored by the City Architects' Department.

83 LAURISTON PLACE, Tollcross
Edinburgh District Council Architects, 1980.

Dark blue brick tenements with string courses recreate the original tenement pattern above heavily rectangular, arcaded shops: totally different, light-harled crow-stepped aesthetic to the rear.

Lauriston Place Fire Station

84 FIRE STATION, Lauriston Place
Robert Morham, City Architect, 1898.

The Arts and Crafts in London had claimed the Fire Station as a building type of their own. This is one of Edinburgh's few approximations, and is a surprisingly graceful red stone building with a slender tower, now decapitated.

85 EXTENSION TO EDINBURGH COLLEGE OF ART, Lauriston Place
Wheeler and Sproson, 1977.

L-shaped development enclosing the College courtyard, in red ashlar and dark stained windows. Geometric shapes, somewhat lacking the boldness of detail that the use of ashlar masonry might have led one to expect.

86 6-44 LAURISTON PLACE
1815-19.

Flatted scheme with front gardens, erected by several builders. Recently restored, with removal of shop fronts, by T. M. Gray and Associates, 1980.

Edinburgh College of Art

ROYAL INFIRMARY EXTENSION,
Lauriston Place
Robert Matthew, Johnson Marshall and Partners, 1981.

Large self-contained block, horizontal in emphasis, capped by steel chimney stack; first phase of a larger redevelopment.

88 CHALMERS HOSPITAL, Lauriston Place
Peddie & Kinnear, 1861-63.

Symmetrical early Italian frontage, Y-plan ward block at rear.

Shona Adam

George Heriot's Hospital **Above:** *north front* **Below:** *elevation by William Playfair showing proposed additional terraces* **Bottom:** *Courtyard interior in 1846, drawn by R W Billings*

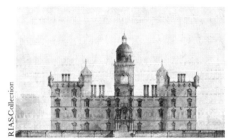

RIAS Collection

89 GEORGE HERIOT'S HOSPITAL,
Lauriston Place
William Wallace and William Ayton,
Master Masons, building 1628-60.

Clock tower and statue of George Heriot added by Robert Mylne in 1693. Original endowment was for the education of *puir fatherless bairns,* established by George Heriot, goldsmith to James VI who christened him *Jingling Geordie.* Scotland's finest early Renaissance building, with plentiful, rich stone carving and tracery displaying a significant German influence. Courtyard plan possibly derived from Serlio, and suggested by the Dean of Rochester, Heriot's nephew, and one of his executors.

McKean

90 ROYAL INFIRMARY, Lauriston Place
David Bryce, with advice from **Florence
Nightingale,** began 1870.

Large corridor and pavilions scheme with
central tower on Fettes model, but more
sparsely detailed. Incorporates William
Adam's George Watson's Hospital of 1738 at
back. Romantic silhouette.

91 MEDICAL SCHOOL, Lauriston Place
Sir R. Rowand Anderson, designed 1875,
completed 1888.

Early Venetian Renaissance, including
vaulted, arcaded, ante-room containing
exhibition of skeletons and animals. A
campanile modelled on St. Mark's at Venice
was planned but not built: a similar one was
imposed onto St. George's West Church
(1879-1881).

92 McEWAN HALL, Teviot Place
Sir R. Rowand Anderson, designed 1875,
revised 1886, completed 1897.

Grandiose early Italianate, echoing
ceremonial hall.

Royal Infirmary, drawn by G. G. Thornby 1912

93 STUDENTS UNION
Sydney Mitchell, 1877.

15th century style palace-block building with
towers of Holyrood-Falkland type: merit of
original concept somewhat diminished by
1906 addition.

94 REID SCHOOL OF MUSIC
David Cousin, 1858.

Finely proportioned, Italian Renaissance
building somewhat putting its more vulgar
neighbours to shame. It houses the Faculty of
Music of the University of Edinburgh.

RCAHMS/Scottish Colorfoto

McEwan Hall, when first complete

George Square, surviving west side

McKean

95 GEORGE SQUARE
Designed and built speculatively by
James Brown, 1763-4.

The square was the first major residential
unit outside the Old Town, and remained
fashionable long after the New Town was
built. Three sides of the Square are now
redeveloped for University Buildings: the
outcry over the demolition of George Square
initiating in a new era in public participation
in planning.

(1) David Hume Tower, 1963; Faculty of
Arts and Social Sciences, 1968.
**Robert Matthew, Johnson-Marshall &
Partners.**
14 storey tower and adjacent development
part of a larger scheme linked by pedestrian
deck.

(2) Appleton Tower, Science Faculty, 1966.
Alan Reiach, Eric Hall & Partners.
Science tower consisting mainly of
laboratories and lecture theatres, with a two-
storey top lit concourse.

Snock

Appleton Tower

(3) University Library, 1967.
Sir Basil Spence, Glover & Ferguson.
Eight storey building, with double height
foyer. Good materials and consistent
detailing, particularly on the exterior, gives
this large library a spare, slightly Japanese,
elegance.

96 ARCHERS' HALL, Buccleuch Street
Alexander Laing, 1776.

The Royal Company of Archers
Headquarters. Originally a small, two storey
and basement, stone box with fine east facing
windows. Later altered and lengthened, with
added Venetian window by Sir R. Rowand
Anderson.

Hunter

University Library

97 BUCCLEUCH PLACE
1772 onwards.

Tall, plain, once fashionable, street still
retaining bow windows are rear and now
mostly converted for University premises.
Note also the **Parish Church** on Buccleuch
Street 1753, renovated by David MacGibbon
1866. Also nearby Hope House, 1770 in what
remains of Hope Park Square, a pleasant
Scots traditioinal building with germanic
decorative gable and curved windowheads,
restored 1978 by Nicholas Groves-Raines as 3
flats. **Buccleuch and Greyfriars Free Church**
is a strikingly original design by the Hays of
Liverpool, 1857-61, whose interior has single-
span laminated trusses.

Inglis Stevens

Archer's Hall

98 STUDENTS CENTRE, Bristo Square
Morris & Steedman, 1976.

Multi-purpose building with shops, society offices, and social facilities, focussed on central 'agora' or concourse, covered by a dome: the intention being that this covered ''outdoor'' quadrangle should have an atmosphere not unlike the square of a Mediterranean village.

99 BRISTO SQUARE
Percy Johnson-Marshall and Associates, 1981.

Formally designed new square in honey coloured blockwork; consequent on replanning of this area.

CHAMBERS STREET

Chambers Street is the mid-Victorian result of slum clearance, inadvertently creating something of an academic enclave. It followed, roughly, the former Jamaica Street and obliterated Argyle and Brown Squares which, together with George's Square and Nicholson Square. Smollett described as ''divers little elegant squares in the English manner'' in 1766.

100 ROYAL SCOTTISH MUSEUM,
Chambers Street
Captain Fowke (Royal Engineers), begun 1861.

Elegant Italianate palace, entrance steps enclosed by projecting wings, with a shallow, brown pantiled roof, corbelled eaves, and serried ranks of twin romanesque windows. Structural cast iron on the Crystal Palace principle is used to create a fine interior, particularly the inspiring entrance hall with its glazed roof and tiers of balconies.

101 HERIOT WATT UNIVERSITY,
Chambers Street
John Chesser 1886-88, incorporating earlier buildings by **David Cousin and John Lessels,** 1873-77.

Squat French château, with florid projecting entrance bay capped by cast-iron crown; details abraded and badly in need of restoration.

102 UNIVERSITY STAFF CLUB,
Chambers Street
Sir Basil Spence, (Hardie Glover,) 1958, in 1875 shell.

Good open plan interior and use of woodwork of the time: one of the best '50s interiors in Edinburgh, with all the spindly details and timberwork that implies: now somewhat altered.

R A Inglis

Student Centre

PSA

Royal Scottish Museum

Edinburgh University Quadrangle

The Upper Library

03 OLD COLLEGE, University of Edinburgh, South Bridge
Robert Adam, 1789.

Planned as two courts, but only the street frontage of the original scheme completed, the main entrance a variation on a Triumphal Arch. The dome above was designed 1886-87 by Sir R. Rowand Anderson, based on that intended by Adam, but greatly enlarged. College completed as single court, by William Playfair, 1818-34, after a competition. His Upper Library is one of the most imposing neo-classical interiors in Scotland, 138 feet long, with an arched, coffered ceiling, and modulated by eleven bays of books. The similarity to a bay of the proposed Temple to the Supreme Being, by the French architect Boullée is striking. There is an elegant gallery. The Upper Museum Hall, now the Talbot Rice Arts Centre, is modelled on Soane's interiors at the Bank of England. Playfair's success was the start of a long enmity with William Burn (who also competed) and subsequently with Burn's assistant, David Bryce, whose election in 1841 to Fellowship of the Architectural Institute of Scotland, Playfair was instrumental in preventing on the grounds that Bryce was only Burn's assistant. Bryce had the last laugh: when Playfair died, his commission for Fettes College (p. 99) went to Bryce.

104 SOUTH COLLEGE STREET CHURCH
Patrick Wilson, 1856.

Tall church facade, in a stump of a street, with a pediment topping a square columned Doric facade. The precision is reminiscent of Alexander Thomson's work in Glasgow. Conch niches.

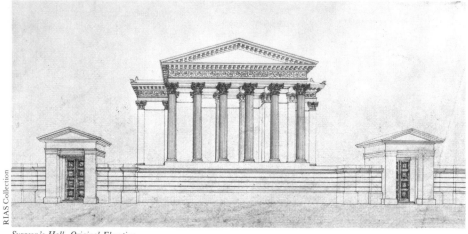

RIAS Collection

Surgeon's Hall, Original Elevation

105 ST. PATRICK'S SCHOOL,
Drummond Street
John Alexander Carfrae, 1905.

Picturesque Scandinavian-Jacobean building developing themes from his 1896-97 school in Preston Street.

106 INFIRMARY GATES, Drummond Street
William Adam, 1738.

The baroque stone gates to the old Royal Infirmary, which was demolished 1879, when replaced by Bryce's new baronial Infirmary in Lauriston Place. Originally in Infirmary Street, the gates were transferred there to form a working approach to David Bryce's former Surgical Hospital of 1848-53, now the University's Natural Philosophy Building. Parts of Adam's Infirmary were re-erected at Redford—the centre part of the attic storey as the lodge to Redford House, the columns as the Covenanters Monument. Enough probably survives to reconstruct the facade.

107 DRUMMOND STREET
and ROXBURGH PLACE

Tall 1790s flatted blocks of some quality including former Episcopal Church in Roxburgh Place, identified by the Venetian windows. Restored by Robert Hurd & Partners 1979-80 for Edinvar Housing Association.

108 EMPIRE THEATRE, 19 Nicolson Street
William and T. R. Milburn, 1927-29.

Insignificant, minimal classical frontage, concealing an impressive, art-deco classical 3-tier auditorium now devoted to bingo.

109 SURGEONS HALL, Nicolson Street
William Playfair, 1832

Pure Greek revivalist temple to medicine, fronted by an Ionic portico flanked by footgates. Impressive museum hall reminiscent of University Library with awesome exhibits. Restored by Robert Hurd and Ian Begg, 1961.

110 31-37 MARSHALL STREET
1765.

Originally H-shaped four storey tenement block, cut in middle to form a street, 1887. Surviving wings rehabilitated for Edinvar Housing Association 1980 by Nicholas Groves-Raines, retaining some original timber and plasterwork.

111 70-76 NICOLSON STREET
Moira and Wann, 1982.

Corner site containing flats for the elderly with shops below: picturesquely roofed corner tower with finial, in pale concrete block with grey brick string courses.

Nicolson Street

12 NICOLSON STREET
Norman Gray and Partners, 1981.

Substantial piece of neo-18th century urban scenery incorporating some of the original buildings, for the Crown Estates Commissioners. Flats above shops in random order, enclosing the curving street.

13 ODEON CINEMA, South Clerk Street
W. E. Trent, 1930.

Fairly typical super cinema of its day, although Trent was not one of the most exciting exponents of the medium. Tiled front, Greek interior with atmospheric sky ceiling. Divided 1981-82, as gently as possible.

14 THE QUEENS HALL, South Clerk Street
Robert Brown, 1823.

Formerly church of Newington and St. Leonards. Galleried interior. Restored as concert hall by Robert Hurd & Partners, 1978.

Hermits and Termits, presentation drawing by Ben Tindall

15 ST. PETER'S EPISCOPAL CHURCH,
Lutton Place
William Slater, 1857-67.

Careful building, beautifully designed in scaled-down Early English Cathedral detailing with circular baptistry, slim tower and curious spire; interesting furnishings.

16 HERMITS & TERMITS,
64 St. Leonards Street
1734.

Panelled interior, gabled front, and harled exterior. After use as railway office and years of neglect, restored, 1981, by Ben Tindall.

17 CARNEGIE COURT, The Pleasance
Ross-Smith & Jamieson, 1966.

Concrete block housing development constructed at a time when low-rise flats such as this were unfashionable. A certain hard, quality, now slightly frayed, but basically an urban scheme of some sensitivity.

Guthrie

The Queen's Hall

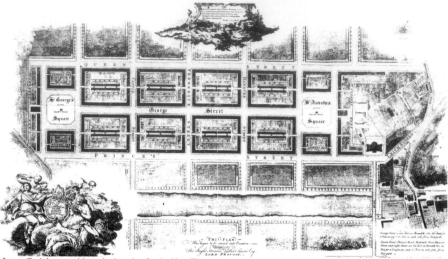

James Craig's competition winning plan for the New Town

The New Town was the result of imaginative daring by Lord Provost Drummond and his Council in the mid 18th century, who obtained Government permission to extend the boundaries of the City by a parallelogram of land on the north side of what was then the Nor' Loch (now Princes Street Gardens). A competition for the New Town's layout was then organised, won in 1766 by an unknown, 22 year old architect, James Craig. His plan consisted of single sided terraces facing over gardens to the south, Princes Street, and the north, Queen Street. Between them lay the main New Town axis then called George Street, terminating at the west in Charlotte Square (originally St. George's Square), and to the east in St. Andrew Square. It was a physical celebration of the unity between England and Scotland, a conceit reflected in the names of the subsidiary streets, Thistle and Rose.

Although building began almost immediately. progress was erratic and sometimes halted when money ran short, as during the Napoleonic Wars. Looking at the New Town now, it is sobering to note that in 1799, (according to the traveller Sarah Murray) *there cannot be much passing and repassing in the new town in summer, for in almost every street the grass grows.* Nor, judging by this comparison between the old and new, made by the American journalist Nathaniel Willis had the situation much improved by 1834. *It is an odd place, Edinburgh. The Old Town and the New are separated by a broad and deep ravine, planted with trees and shrubbery. A more striking contrast than exists between these two parts of the same city could hardly be imagined. On one side a succession of splendid squares, elegant granite houses, broad and well paved streets, columns, statues and clean side walks, thinly promenaded and by the well-dressed exclusively,—a kind of wholly grand and half deserted city which has been built too ambitiously for the population, and, on the other, and antique*

wilderness of streets and "wynds," so narrow and lofty as to shut out much of the light of heaven; a thronging, busy and particularly dirty population; sidewalks almost impossible from children and other respected nuisances; and altogether between the irregular and massive architecture, and the unintelligible jargon agonizing the air about you, a most outstanding and strange city.

By 1970, the New Town had passed its 200 birthday with many of its buildings visibly deteriorating badly. A fabric survey was undertaken by the Edinburgh Architectural Association, followed by an international conference, the outcome being the establishment of the Edinburgh New Town Conservation Committee which, with grant aid from the Government, is stimulating and overseeing a major programme of repair and rehabilitation. In their headquarters at 13a Dundas Street, there is an exhibition gallery and bookshop illustrating techniques of conservation.

PRINCES STREET

One of Europe's most celebrated streets, primarily for its aspect to the gardens and castle, this view itself being protected only after a legal battle. The Mound was formed by spoil excavated from the New Town. Although in 1802 the street was *a far extended row of houses pretty uniformly arranged,* by 1840 the street's uniformity had been splintered by the arrival of commerce and clubs. Robert Louis Stevenson thought the result *a terrace of palaces,* but the 20th century judgement was harsher. In 1960 Moray McLaren condemned it as *one of the most chaotically tasteless streets in the United Kingdom;* and that prevailing view lead to much of the subsequent destruction and desire for a new uniformity, manifesting itself in the Princes Street panel guidelines (see later).

Register House

DUKE OF WELLINGTON STATUE,
Princes Street
Sir John Steell, 1852.

Equestrian statue completed by the anniversary of Waterloo 1852. The Iron Duke in bronze by Steell, as wags had it.

18 REGISTER HOUSE, Princes Street
Robert Adam. Started in 1774.

Houses the National Records in possibly the finest classical building in Edinburgh: two storeys with concealed basement, the ground floor rusticated. Central, projecting Corinthian portico capped by the dome behind, somewhat as Adam had done at Kedleston Hall. Pavilions at each end, pilastered, balustraded, and topped by cupolas. Splendid domed hall within. In use by 1778, after delays due to lack of funds—northern third completed with Adam plan altered by Robert Reid, 1822-34.

Adjacent Register House is by **Robert Matheson** 1856-62, with an iron galleried interior and domed centre.

19 BURTONS, Princes Street
Sir John James Burnet, 1906-7 and 1923-25.

Sumptuous Edwardian building and Edinburgh's first steel-framed store, recently reconditioned.

20 SCOTT MONUMENT, Princes Street
George Meikle Kemp, 1844.

The winner of an open architectural competition. *The odds were always against the nonentity who had no partisans on the committee, and Kemp wisely masked his obscurity under the convenient cloak of a romantic pseudonym. . . It was no small thing for a modest country joiner to embark on the design and construction of such a vast and intricate pile of Gothic masonry. In a sense it is*

The Scott Monument in 1891

perhaps the most naively philistine structure in the country. (Architectural Prospect 1929). Original drawings and model on exhibition. Kemp was a self-taught architect, who had worked for a time in Burn's office. The monument is the only significant known building by him; he drowned in the Union Canal whilst the monument was being constructed. The statue of Sir Walter Scott by Sir John Steell was installed in 1846.

121 OLD WAVERLEY HOTEL,
43-46 Princes Street
John Armstrong, 1883.

Free Renaissance hotel building with
mansard roof, complementing Jenners across
South St. David Street, but lacking its
panache.

122 JENNERS, Princes Street
William Hamilton Beattie, 1895.

Opulent store redolent of the late Victorian
period: last carriage-trade survivor in Princes
Street, with an exterior gorged with Baroque
detail. Mock Jacobean central well inside.
Beattie was also the architect of the Station
Hotel for the North British Railway, of which
Jenner was chairman.

123 BRITISH HOME STORES, 64 Princes Street
**Robert Matthew, Johnson-Marshall &
Partners,** 1968.

Good exemplar of the now-abandoned *Princess
Street Panel* recommendations aimed at
creating a new, 20th century, urban
uniformity: first floor walkway, two
projecting upper storeys, and shops at ground
floor.

124 ROYAL SCOTTISH ACADEMY,
Princes Street
William Playfair, 1832.

Enlarged by him in 1833-36 greatly
improving and balancing the composition.
Massive, squat Doric temple, with a
profusion of carved and incised stone. Queen
Victoria's statue, over portico, by Sir John
Steell. Fine, raised, sequence of rooflit
galleries inside, reconstructed in convincing
neo Greek with re-inforced concrete roofs by
W. T. Oldrieve, 1910.

Shona Adam

Jenners

Above and below: *Royal Scottish Academy*

Joe Rock

Joe Rock

Above and below: *The National Gallery*

Shona Adams

125 *NATIONAL GALLERY,* Mound
William Playfair, 1845.

Exterior treatment of RSA to north here ingeniously turned round: principal porticos now on long side, whereas facades have twin projecting porticos with entrance in antis. Exterior of blind walls of shallow pilasters in pink stone broached by tall Ionic porticos plainer than the RSA and thereby more elegant. Interior gallery sequence more flamboyant with Corinthian columned screens (an Edwardian embellishment) between the galleries. Classical scholars note that Doric columns (RSA) imply authority and masculinity; whilst Ionic (National Gallery) convey a reflective, matronly attitude. Perhaps the architecture is trying to tell us something about the character of those two institutions. New underground gallery by Property Services Agency, 1978.

126 *ALLAN RAMSAY STATUE,*
Princes Street Gardens
Sir John Steell, 1865, pedestal designed by **David Bryce.**

127 *NEW CLUB,* 85 Princes Street
Alan Reiach (Stuart Renton), 1966.

Replaces the old club by Burn (1834) and Bryce (1859). Marvellous interiors including partially reconstructed, original, dining room. Exterior in accord with planner's requirements: two floors of shops below, with (unused) first floor walkway. Club projects above walkway, clad in large panels of bluish granite, vertically applied. By far the best result of the *Princes Street Panel* recommendations.

Snoek

The New Club

Joe Rock

Debenhams

McKean

St. John's Church, drawn by Thomas Shepherd

Hunter

Royal Bank of Scotland, West End Branch

128 DEBENHAMS, Princes Street
1882 (and later).

Rowand Anderson's asymmetrical, red roofed and polished stone Conservative Club restored by Simpson & Brown (1978), who moved the grand stair to the rear; otherwise gutted and recast as a store by Ketley, Goold and Clark who also designed the glass frontage to the east linking to former Liberal Club, the upper floors of which have also been absorbed into the scheme. First circular glass-enclosed lifts in Edinburgh.
Wallis's is French renaissance in style, by John Lessels 1869, with a cast iron galleried shop interior.

129 ST. JOHN'S CHURCH, Princes Street
William Burn, 1816, chancel **Peddie & Kinnear,** 1879.

Pleasant, robustly detailed Gothic revival building: café in restored under-croft. Notable fan-vaulted interior much more spacious than one would expect from the exterior; interesting memorial, and reredos with W. B. Simpson tilework. John Ruskin thought the Church simply *beautiful.*

130 138 PRINCES STREET and 2-8 SOUTH CHARLOTTE STREET
Sir T. Duncan Rhind 1903 and **J. D. Cairns** 1924 and 1935.

Originally L-shaped with two crowded Baroque gables facing Princes Street and South Charlotte Street. The corner building between was replaced in 1924 with matching gable on splayed corner, curtain-walled facades with bronze panels between; further addition to north 1935 with art-deco staircase.

131 WEST END BRANCH, ROYAL BANK OF SCOTLAND, Princes Street
Sir Basil Spence, Glover & Ferguson 1979.

Preservation of Victorian palazzo facade of some elegance by John MacLauchlan, 1888, surrounded by banded stone and glass like a butterfly in a case. The interior has fine views, a superb staircase and ashlar lift-shaft. Exterior a test case of the worth of partial conservation. A lost opportunity when viewed down Lothian Road; much more satisfactorily viewed from the pavement where MacLauchlan's details still give pleasure.

32 CALEDONIAN HOTEL, Rutland Street
1898-1902 by **J. M. Peddie & G.
Washington Browne** over 1880s station
substructure by **Kinnear & Peddie.**

Originally a railway hotel. A wonderfully
blousy intrusion into West End Edinburgh.
V-shaped, in gigantic combination of the
Dutch Baroque gables with French roofs,
above large-scaled columned and friezed
lower storeys; all in blushing pockmarked
sandstone.

33 RUTLAND SQUARE
Designed by **Archibald Elliot,** 1819, partially
revised and built by **John Tait** 1830-40.

Only New Town square south of Princes
Street, smaller in scale than the others, and
somewhat hemmed in by commerce.
Technically, it is part of the later Western
New Town, along with Atholl Crescent (see
p. 71). No. 15—Headquarters of Royal
Incorporation of Architects in Scotland,
RIAS Gallery and bookshop; also home of the
Edinburgh Architectural Association.

Joe Rock

The Caledonian Hotel

34 ST. GEORGE'S WEST CHURCH,
Shandwick Place
David Bryce, 1869.

Confident, large scale Baroque building (à la
Sir John Vanbrugh) on the corner of Stafford
Street, considerably altered by addition of
Venetian campanile by Sir Rowand
Anderson, 1879. A Gibbsian interior
translated into cast-iron.

35 WILKIE'S, 53-61 Shandwick Place
Reid & Forbes, 1937.

Stone fronted, symmetrical building with
heavy neo-Egyptian '30s details above the
obtrusive shop fascia. The central entrance
has recently been relocated, and the design
suffers from the loss of its canopy. Reid and
Forbes were responsible for a number of
vaguely Art-Deco schools in Edinburgh.

**36 QUEENSFERRY STREET/SHANDWICK
PLACE CORNER**
Sydney Mitchell & Wilson, 1901, ground
floor altered later by **Sir Matthew
Ochterlony** 1938-40.

Stone commercial block turning the corner
with an underscaled cupola, shallow stone
details, and curvilinear wallhead gables. The
whole assembly would have been improved
by some of the Glaswegian guts then visible
on the West Coast.

37 HOPE STREET/QUEENSFERRY STREET
1790s.

Attractive freestanding block terminating
Charlotte Square flank. Steep roof, twin
shallow bay windows. Epitomises native Scots
architecture sprouting like a weed through
tarmac into the international classicism of
Charlotte Square.

RCAHMS/Edinburgh Central Library

St. George's Church, with the original proposal for the steeple

Hope Street/Queensferry Street

RCAHMS

Above: *Original drawing for North and South side of Charlotte Square*
Below: *North side of Charlotte Square*

McKean

138 CHARLOTTE SQUARE
Robert Adam, 1791.

The north side finished in the 18th century, the rest (with some alterations) in the early 19th century. Individual terraced houses sublimated within monumental palace facades which had a strong influence on the later New Towns.

Charlotte Square later became the haunt of lawyers and doctors:—Sir Robert Lorimer wrote scathingly: *I regard it as being just as important for me to be in the centre of things as for a doctor to be in Charlotte Square. You want to keep in touch with all these pot-bellied W. S. and people.*

Lord Cockburn lived at no. 14, from which he wrote: *Whatever Mr Cockburn was, His Majesty's Solicitor General is a decorous person, arrayed in solemn black, with a demure visage, an official ear and evasive voice, suspicious palate, ascetic blood and flinty heart. There is a fellow very like him who traverses the Pentlands in a dirty grey jacket, white hat and long pole. **That's** not the Solicitor-General, that's Cocky.* An excellent illustration of the Jekyll and Hyde syndrome. The Scottish Arts Council occupies no. 19; no. 5 is the Headquarters of the National Trust for Scotland; no. 7 their 'Georgian House' (open to visitors); and no 6. is the official residence of the Secretary of State for Scotland. **Guide book to no. 7 available.**

Charlotte Square

St. George's Church

ST. GEORGE'S CHURCH, Charlotte Square
Robert Reid, 1811.

An unexciting church, plainer than Adam's original (rather French design à la Pantheon in Paris), with a taller dome and a recessed rather than projecting, portico. Consolidation and conversion to West Register by DoE architects from 1964.

139 127 GEORGE STREET
c. 1790.

Restoration of original New Town buildings, by removal of later shop-fronts and restoration of front area. By Robert Hurd and Partners, 1975.

140 CHURCH OF SCOTLAND OFFICES,
117-121 George Street
Sydney Mitchell and E. A. Jamieson, 1911, extended eastwards 1929.

Unusual fusion of Scandinavian, Edwardian London and Egyptian influences: Greek Doric arcaded ground floor of granite, chanelled upper facade with eaves gallery, and two-tier mansard roof.

North Castle Street

141 115 GEORGE STREET
James Nisbet, c. 1790.

Flashy Corinthian pilastered house, survivor of group of three with some good interior work as befits a building designed by a plasterer. Restored to its original external appearance, Covell Mathews Partnership, 1979-80.

142 NORTH CASTLE STREET
1790; 39-43 of particular interest, possibly by **Alexander Crawford,** completed in 1793.

Constructed as two, two storey with basement, main door flats, topped by a single flat running across the entire building, entered from the central doorway. Underscaled pedimented centrepiece, flanked by shallow, symmetrical bows. Appealing superimposition of classical architecture onto the more sedate local traditions. No. 39 was the home of Sir Walter Scott from 1802-1826.

Bank of Scotland

143 BANK OF SCOTLAND,
101-103 George Street
J. M. Dick Peddie, 1884.

Italian Renaissance Palace with splendid banking hall, restored along with Georgian house on west by Robert Hurd and Partners 1978; house on east built new, approximately reproducing the appearance of the first generation New Town house on the site until 1885.

144 FREEMASONS' HALL, 96 George Street
A. Hunter Crawford, 1912.

Restrained Renaissance facade: sumptuous interior with clerestoried hall.

145 93 GEORGE STREET
Thomas Hamilton, 1833.

Recast for Melrose the tea-merchant in a unique regency essay: note particularly the verandah, the top storey of roundheaded windows, and the cast iron columns allegedly (and originally) supporting the balcony above. The building in Edinburgh which most resembled the contemporary work of John Nash in London. Restored by Robert Hurd & Partners, 1980-82; no. 95, also restored by them, is by David Bryce, 1840.

146 NATIONAL WESTMINSTER BANK,
(Star House), 80 George Street
Sir John J. Burnet, 1903.

Built as department store, tall Edwardian Baroque with caryatid eaves gallery between domelets. Early-modern facade facing lane at rear. Interior reconstructed and ground floor facade restored by Ian Burke Associates.

147 71 GEORGE STREET and 36, 38 NORTH FREDERICK STREET
T. P. Marwick, 1908.

Characterless Edwardian baroque with splayed corner rising into a dome.

148 BANK OF SCOTLAND, 69 George Street
Sir George Washington Browne, 1905.

Francois Ier, curved corner, with good sculptures at the entrance and ground floor windows.

149 BANK OF SCOTLAND, 62-66 George Street
David Bryce, 1874-78 completed by his nephew **John.**

Bryce's last Italianate banking palace with a notable, recently refurbished telling room.

150 ASSEMBLY ROOMS and MUSIC HALL,
George Street
John Henderson, 1784-1787.

Portico 1818 and Music Hall to rear 1843 by William Burn. Originally very plain, and

Joe Rock

93 George Street

unpopular thereby. Enlivened by pedimented portico encompassing the entire pavement, and later with the insertion of the semi-bowed orchestra bay projecting into it, by David Bryce. Typical First New Town houses on each side. (c. 1780).

151 45 GEORGE STREET
Recast in 1829 for **William Blackwood.**

Imposing Ionic shopfront signifying the former status of Blackwoods, and the current status of a French bank.

Assembly Rooms

Inglis Stevens

52 *CLYDESDALE BANK,* 29-31 George Street
David Bryce, 1841.

Extended down Hanover Street, 1847. Corinthian pilastraded frontage with end porticos, subsidiary pilastrade threaded through the giant one in the David Hamilton manner. In 1853 John Ruskin commented savagely: *your decorations are just as monotonous as your simplicities. How many Corinthian and Doric columns do you think there are in your banks, and post offices, institutions, and I know not what else, one exactly like another?—and yet you expect to be interested!*

53 *EDINBURGH SAVINGS BANK,*
28-30 Hanover Street
William Paterson of Oldrieve Bell and Paterson, 1939.

Unfriendly bank building in blank American style, with giant Ionic portico; fastidiously detailed.

Clydesdale Bank

54 *MERCHANT COMPANY OFFICES,*
20-22 Hanover Street
David Bryce Junior, 1865-66, original scheme completed **T. P. Marwick** 1901.

Unspectacular, well detailed, bay-windowed, Italianate facade whose southern portico was removed in course of restoration by Leslie Graham Macdougall. Halls to rear provide interesting contrast of early Victorian classicism and Edwardian Baroque.

55 *ST. ANDREW'S CHURCH,* George Street
Major Andrew Fraser, 1785.

Spire, 1789, designed by William Sibbald and executed by Alexander Stevens. Competition-winning church possibly copied from an Italian original. Corinthian portico fronting oval auditorium with fine plaster work on the flat ceiling. Flat ceiling itself somewhat at odds with the deliberate attempt to make the exterior similar to an eliptical Pantheon, in its pre-spire days. The church was the scene of the Disruption at the Church of Scotland General Assembly in 1843.

56 *ROYAL SOCIETY BUILDING,*
22-24 George Street
David Bryce, 1843.

Refined Italian Renaissance with Doric porches and first floor Corinthian aedicules. Interior under reconstruction 1982, Robert Hurd and Partners.

57 *ROYAL BANK OF SCOTLAND,*
14 George Street
David Rhind, 1847; sculptor, **A. H. Ritchie.**

Yet another Temple to mammon: Corinthian portico, modelled on Playfair's original scheme for the Surgeons' Hall. Domed atrium of superimposed orders. Corinthian banking hall further embellished by Sydney Mitchell in 1888.

St. Andrew's Church

158 GEORGE HOTEL, George Street
David Bryce, 1840.

Enlarged to present form by MacGibbon & Ross 1879 as Caledonian Insurance Building. Corinthian colonnaded at first and second floor. Impressive business hall at back, now minus some columns to accommodate more diners. Upper floors always an hotel.

159 ST. ANDREW SQUARE

Eastern end of George Street, balancing Charlotte Square to the West, the ensemble being the spine of the New Town. The Royal Bank headquarters, formerly the Dundas mansion, takes the place of what would have been the eastern equivalent of St. George's Church in Charlotte Square: an early example of the triumph of land ownership over good planning.

Standard Life

HOPETOUN MONUMENT
1824-34 by **Thomas Campbell**.

Equestrian statue of John Hope, Earl of Hopetoun; inscription by Sir Walter Scott.

MELVILLE MONUMENT
William Burn, 1821.

Glorification of the most powerful Scotsman of his time, Henry Dundas, Viscount Melville. Lord Cockburn described him as, in 1800, the *absolute dictator of Scotland*. Lord Macauley, thought it *very much better than the man deserved. It is impossible to look at it without being reminded of the fate which the original most richly merited.* Statue by Robert Forrest 1828. Consultant foundation advice from Robert Stevenson, grandfather of Robert Louis.

STANDARD LIFE ASSURANCE COMPANY,
corner George Street/St. Andrew Square **Michael Laird & Partners** in association with **Sir Robert Matthew**.

This substantial continuing development frames the elegant original corner building by J. M. Peddie & G. Washington Browne 1897-1901, re-using a Sir John Steell pediment from previous building and clearly influenced by the Dundas mansion. George Street facade is 1978: St. Andrew Square facade is 1968; and just behind St. Andrew's Church can be seen the 1964 green curtain-walled extension.

2 North St. David's Street

2 NORTH ST. DAVID'S STREET
Reiach and Hall, 1969.

Infill office development characterised by a series of rectangular bays, with shallow pilasters at top, and a strongly modelled base.

THISTLE COURT, Thistle Street
John Young, 1767.

Rubble built, modest semi-detached houses facing each other across a garden. The easterly preserves nice rustic pediment above the doors and fine projecting lamp. Earliest surviving construction in the New Town, showing nothing of the composite grandeur that was to follow.

Above: *Royal Bank of Scotland, drawn by Thomas Shepherd* **Below:** *Interior*

21/22 ST. ANDREW SQUARE/ NORTH ST. DAVID'S STREET
1772.

Plain Scots flatted block, possibly formerly harled, with ground floor of 1840. Now scrubbed clean for new IBM Headquarters in Scotland by Covell Matthews & Partners with Rock Townsend, 1980. Once home of Earl of Buchan, whence he founded the Society of Antiquaries. Restoration of the austere North St. David's Street facade a joy to behold.

23 ST. ANDREW SQUARE
David Bryce, 1846.

Small, rich palazzo, formerly yet another bank.

26 ST. ANDREW SQUARE
Sir William Chambers, 1770-72.

Facade remodelled 1840. Some interesting details within, although deepened in plan at back by Kinnear & Peddie

SCOTTISH EQUITABLE INSURANCE BUILDING, 28 St. Andrew Square
J. M. Dick Peddie & Sir George Washington Browne, 1897.

English Jacobean with Bolsover gables and some French Renaissance touches. Under reconstruction by Michael Laird and Partners, 1982.

ROYAL BANK OF SCOTLAND,
St. Andrew Square
Sir William Chambers 1772-74.

Designed as a private house for Sir Laurence Dundas. A building that achieves its status by understatement; tall, three storey, five bay house, no basement, with shallow, three bay, Corinthian pilastered entrance, fine frieze and projecting cornice. The Telling Room by Peddie & Kinnear 1857, has an impressive iron dome with glazed star-shaped coffers.

35 ST. ANDREW SQUARE
Robert Adam, 1769. (surviving drawings not scheme built).

Designed, along with no. 36, (built by John Young in 1781) as symmetrical pavilions on either side of the Dundas Mansion. Facade crushed by four giant Ionic columns, reaching through two storeys, continued as pilasters in the attic, each of which is capped by an urn.

38 St Andrew Square

38 and 39 ST. ANDREW SQUARE
David Bryce, 1851-52.

Now the Bank of Scotland, but formerly the British Linen Bank. A sumptuous Roman facade with disengaged Corinthian columns, each topped by a statue by A. H. Ritchie. Interior contains magnificent grand staircase and top lit telling room, with granite columns and a tiled floor, now carpeted over.

Scottish Provident Institution

SCOTTISH PROVIDENT INSTITUTION,
St. Andrew Square
Rowand Anderson, Kininmonth & Paul,
1961.

Horizontal, glazed office areas, flanked by a solid, vertically proportioned service tower. A contrast in planes, between solids and voids, using only two principal materials—a bluish glass and polished stone. The result is an elegant and sophisticated design: one of the best infill buildings of its period in Britain.

160 ROYAL BANK STATIONARY WAREHOUSE, West Register Street
W. Hamilton Beattie, 1864.

Lavish Venetian Gothic with angles splayed to ease traffic congestion in narrow street.

161 THE CAFE ROYAL, West Register Street
Robert Paterson, 1862.

Opulent corner-block, with fine late Victorian plasterwork, stained glass and ceramic murals, installed by J. McIntyre Henry. Interiors imply a hedonism uncharacteristic in Edinburgh, which may explain why it is so well tucked away from the public gaze.

Cafe Royal

Joe Rock

Waterloo Place

62 WATERLOO PLACE
Archibald Elliot, 1815.

Acts as a formal, classical gateway to Regent
Road, in deliberate contrast to the ruggedness of
Calton Hill behind. Designed as near
symmetrical terraces with tetrastyle Ionic
porticos at the pavilions flanking the approach.
General Post Office at North Bridge corner a
grandiose palazzo by Robert Mathieson,
1861-65, further aggrandised by W. T. Oldrieve,
1907-10; on the site of the former Theatre Royal
and Shakespeare Square.

REGENT BRIDGE
Archibald Elliot, 1815.

A War Memorial doubling as a bridge: Ionic
screens with Corinthian arch in middle, over
giant semi circular span carrying Waterloo Place
over Calton Road.

63 CALTON OLD BURIAL GROUND

Contains many interesting monuments but in
particular that to the political martyrs (Thomas
Hamilton 1844), Robert Adam's austere,
circular memorial to David Hume 1777,
(inspired by the tomb of Theodoric at
Ravenna), and the American Civil War
memorial by George E. Bissett of New York,
1893.

64 GOVERNOR'S HOUSE,
Regent Road
Archibald Elliot, 1815.

Only survival of the picturesque Old Calton
gaol, awaiting a new use: *One of the finest sites in
the world* wrote Sir Rowand Anderson, *covered
with a toy castle devoid of expression and utterly
meaningless; the towers and battlements are mere make-
believes.* The remainder of the gaol was
demolished for the Scottish Office headquarters,
St. Andrew's House (see below).

McKean

St. Andrew's House

165 ST. ANDREW'S HOUSE
Thomas Tait, 1934-39.

On the site of the former Calton Jail;
Scotland's most prominent 1930s building. It
has the brooding, authoritarian characteristics of the secure headquarters of an
occupying Power. The fineness of its 1930s
details—front lamps, canopies, stair towers
etc., does little to lighten the effect, which has
been compared to those heavy Art Deco
clocks which squat on mantlepieces.

RIAS Collection

Drawing No. 2 by Henry Kerr to accompany the 1907 appeal to complete the National Monument

166 CALTON HILL

Calton Hill, commented Sir Patrick Geddes, with its strange medley of monuments is a museum of the battle of styles and a permanent evidence showing how the town planners of one generation cannot safely count upon continuance by those of the next. A study of the appropriateness of the building form to purpose demonstrates the extent to which the choices were made on architectural grounds: a circular classical temple to Burns, the ploughboy poet? A half-complete Greek temple to celebrate military victory? What matters in Calton Hill is the skyline. *Albert,* recorded Queen Victoria *said he felt sure the Acropolis could not be finer.*

CALTON HILL (Street)

Picturesque later 18th century terrace stepped down a rocky slope. Nos. 16-18 recently restored to original form by Robert Hurd & Partners for Cockburn Conservation Trust 1981. A further block facing west built anew by same architects for Viewpoint Housing Association, re-uses a doorpiece from George Square. The resultant, pleasant, rural 18th century Laird's house may be seen as Conservation's diminutive David against the Goliath of the St. James' Centre which crouches across the sadly widened road.

NATIONAL MONUMENT
C. R. Cockerell (with William Playfair), 1822.

Proposal for the National Memorial of the Napoleonic Wars; foundation stone laid during George IV's visit to Edinburgh. Designed as a church whose exterior was intended to be a replica of the Parthenon—unfortunately, the scale was such that the money ran to only twelve columns.

Joe Rock

The National Monument today

The Royal High School

DUGALD STEWART'S MONUMENT
William Playfair, 1832.

Open Corinthian peristyle, modelled on 4th century monument of Lysicrates at Athens, erected to celebrate his choir's success in a competition.

OLD OBSERVATORY
James Craig, 1776.

Planned as the City Observatory with advice from Robert Adam. It is one of Craig's very few suviving buildings: an extraordinary example of ham-fisted, picturesque, castellated Gothic, by the inspirer of the severely classical New Town.

NEW OBSERVATORY
William Playfair, 1818.

Cruciform classical temple with central dome, constructed on summit of the precinct. Its existence was largely due to the activities of the architect's uncle, Professor Playfair, the eminent mathematician and natural philosopher, and President of the recently formed Astronomical Institution.

PLAYFAIR'S MONUMENT
William Playfair, 1826.

Classical cenotaph (memorial to Professor Playfair), forming the corner to the Observatory precinct wall. Modelled on the 1st century tomb of Theron at Agrigento and on the Lion Tomb at Cnidos.

NELSON'S MONUMENT

An up-ended stone telescope, designed shortly after Trafalgar by Robert Burn, father of the more celebrated architect, William, but not completed until 1816 by R. & R. Dickson.

167 ROYAL HIGH SCHOOL
Thomas Hamilton, 1825-29

A building of international stature that most justified Edinburgh's nickname *Athens of the North.* Some evidence that the design was considered integrally with the proposed National Monument on the hill above, so as to create an Edinburgh Acropolis. The central Doric temple contains the splendid oval hall (later, proposed Debating Chamber), with shallow coffered ceiling, and cast iron columns supporting the balcony. Converted, 1976, to home for the Scottish Assembly.

BURNS MONUMENT
Thomas Hamilton, completed 1830.

Circular Greek temple with Corinthian peristyle. Currently under restoration.

The Burns Monument

McKean

Royal Terrace

168 1-34 REGENT TERRACE, 1-19 CARLTON TERRACE and 1-40 ROYAL TERRACE
William Playfair, from 1819.

The eastern development from Edinburgh, including Calton Hill and the upper part of Leith Walk, was subject of another competition. The general principles followed, particularly the advantageous use of topography and contour, and the integration of trees, were those of William Stark, a fine Glasgow architect who died soon afterwards. Sir Walter Scott mentioned *the loss of poor Stark, with whom more genius has died than is left behind in the collected universality of Scottish architects.* Cockburn, more simply, called him *the best modern architect that Scotland had produced.* Playfair, who had once been a pupil of Stark's, followed the Stark recommendations closely, and won the commission. The New Town terraces on the eastern slopes of Calton Hill are more modest than contemporary structures on the Moray Estate-except for Royal Terrace whose procession of Ionic and Corinthian colonnades is the grandest of them all. Communal garden behind.

169 LADY GLENORCHY'S CHURCH,
Greenside Place
1844-46.

Large plain classical auditorium to which the collegiate Tudor facade was added by John Henderson 1846.

170 1-5 and 6-10 BLENHEIM PLACE
William Playfair, 1819.

Roman Doric corner block, linked to Baxter's Place by a quadrant portico. The apparently single storey section, is the uppermost floor of several storeys to the rear of humbler dwellings, built in the steep hollow of Greenside.

Kelly

Baxter's Place

171 1-8 BAXTER'S PLACE
John Baxter, 1800.

A speculative terraced house development later mutilated by addition of shops. Once home of Robert Stevenson, the lighthouse engineer, and grandfather to Robert Louis Stevenson. Western two thirds now restored as offices, 1981, by Robert Hurd and Partners. Europa Nostra Award.

172 PLAYHOUSE THEATRE,
18-22 Greenside Place
John Fairweather, 1927-29.

Vast inter-war classical cinema theatre seating 3,000, on a steeply falling site, recently brought back into use and refurbished with Art Deco touches by Lothian Region Council architects' department.

73 1-5 GAYFIELD PLACE
and 33 GAYFIELD SQUARE
James Begg, 1791.

Gayfield Place is conceived as an unity,
flanked by two pleasant, shallow bows, with
Venetian windows: central block capped by
twin diminutive pediments. South side of
Gayfield Square contains some of the earliest
villas in Edinburgh.

74 MIDDLEFIELD, Leith Walk
1795-96.

An ashlar-fronted suburban villa with
Venetian windows and a central gable pierced
by windows, mouldering gently behind later
street-front tenements.

75 GAYFIELD HOUSE, East London Street
Charles and William Buttar, 1763.

Toy-like country house, perched on a raised
ground floor, and sporting urns, Ionic
doorway, central pediment, and curvilinear
chimney gables on flanks. Originally had a
landscaped park running up to Leith Walk,
developed as Gayfield Square from 1790.

76 CATHOLIC APOSTOLIC CHURCH,
London Street
Sir Robert Rowand Anderson, 1876.

Neo-Norman in style, with a vast apsed
interior, and murals by Phoebe Traquair.

77 ST. MARY'S CHURCH, Bellevue Crescent
Thomas Brown, 1826.

Portico of six Corinthian columns, with ranks
of them lining the slender tower, capped by a
domelet of Robert Smirke type. Galleried
interior with original pulpit.

78 BELLEVUE CRESCENT
1802.

Planned by Reid and Sibbald, elevations of
southern half by Thomas Bonnar, northern
by David Cousin, following Bonnar's design,
but stepped in slope. Giant Ionic pilasters and
a pleasing symmetry.

Top: *Gayfield Place* **Above:** *Middlefield* **Below:**
Gayfield House **Below left:** *Bellevue Crescent*

179 CHURCH OF NAZARENE,
Broughton Street/Albany Street
David Skae, 1816.

Idiosyncratic, square fronted church with
projecting porch and fanlight, designed as
terminal pavilion to a street, Venetian
window, and swags on side wall. Now
converted by Baron Bercott and Associates to
Building Society offices.

180 ALBANY STREET
Possibly by **George Winton.**
Feued from 1798.

The unfashionable side of the New Town: a
delightful district of smaller houses, still
retaining their elegance, fanlights, pediments
and doorcases. A quarter of artists, architects
and Housing Associations. Note particularly
Offices, Albany Lane, converted from
stables by Campbell and Arnott: includes
exhibition gallery.

181 BROUGHTON PLACE CHURCH
Archibald Elliot, 1821.

Greek Doric portico. Interior lavishly recast
with Romanesque influences, John Paterson,
1870.

182 ST. PAUL'S and ST. GEORGE'S
EPISCOPAL CHURCH, York Place,
corner Broughton Street
Archibald Elliot, 1816-18,
chancel **Kinnear & Peddie,** 1892.

Ambitious neo-perpendicular church of a
college chapel type.

183 ST. GEORGE'S CHAPEL, York Place
James Adam, 1794.

Unusual, rib vaulted, plaster octagon
survives as part of a commercial showroom:
heavy facade mutilatedly unrecognisable.

184 YORK PLACE
Complete in 1800.

Wide extension to Queen Street containing
some of the best surviving, untouched, New
Town buildings. No. 5b, designed by James
Adam, and completed in 1794. No. 32,
completed 1795, was Sir Henry Raeburn's
studio 1798-1809. Thomas Hamilton lived in
no. 57.

The Portrait Gallery in 1910

PSA

185 SCOTTISH NATIONAL PORTRAIT
GALLERY
Sir R. Rowand Anderson, 1886-90.

The Doge's palace from Venice in red
sandstone, the long, main facade rather weak.
The composition has a certain industrial feel
about it. Larger corner tourelles were
planned, but encroached too much on
pavement. Two storeyed central hall with
ambulatory and tapestry-like murals by
William Hole.

Joe Rock

The Royal College of Physicians

66 2-67 QUEEN STREET
Generally completed by 1780.

Queen Street was the northern equivalent of Princes Street in Craig's original plan. Its dimensions are somewhat distended by its eastern extension into York Place, and Western extension into Albyn Place and St. Colme Street. It was along this street that John Ruskin sternly counted 688 identical windows *altogether devoid of any relief or decoration* in 1853, as an example of the monotony of the New Town.

No. 11 was described, in 1815, as *a very gloomy old barrack . . . on the front of which the sun never shone, and which was so built against behind there was no free circulation of air through it.*

No. 8 completed 1771, by Robert Adam for Lord Chief Baron Orde, and contains superb plaster ceilings.

No. 9 Royal College of Physicians, 1845, by Thomas Hamilton; statues by A. H. Ritchie. Exterior shows remarkable invention within the confines of a classical terraced frontage: a pedimented portico to the central window on the first floor, flanked and topped by statues, rests upon the flat portico to the main entrance beneath. Impressive interior and staircase; large Corinthian-columned hall doubled in size by David Bryce to Imperial grandeur, who also added the fine library Hall in 1877.

E

McKean

Above: *Heriot Row.* **Below:** *Heriot Row as planned*

RGAHMS/Heriot Trust

187 NORTHERN NEW TOWN

Planned by **Robert Reid and William Sibbald,** 1801-2.

Abercromby Place, Heriot Row and the main axis of **Great King Street—Drummond Place —London Street** were all designed by Reid, (the latter with modifications by Thomas Bonnar), and the rest mainly by Thomas Bonnar and Thomas Brown.
Great King Street is by far the grandest—its majestic scale deliberately enhanced by the domesticity of (originally) middle-class Northumberland Street (south) and (originally) artisan-class Cumberland Street (to the north).

188 ROYAL BANK OF SCOTLAND COMPUTER CENTRE, Dundas Street
Michael Laird and Partners, 1980.

Ziggurat, gable end to the street, of honey coloured stone and dark glass. Recycled waste heat from the computers, provides all the heating required for the building.

Inglis Stevens

Great King Street

Moray Place

McKean

189 MORAY ESTATE
James Gillespie Graham from 1822.

Designed for the Earl of Moray, Randolph Place, Ainslie Place and Moray Place are all connected by Great Stuart Street and cleverly linked to earlier developments. Moray Place, in which the Earl had his house at no. 28, was the cynosure of the development; a twelve sided circus—the largest in Edinburgh—consisting of a series of ponderous pedimented and columned mansion facades, above a rusticated floor, linked by plain buildings. Important interior by William Playfair at no. 47. The estate is linked, on the north, by Doune Terrace, (Gillespie Graham 1822) to Gloucester Place, the western extremity of Reid and Sibbald's central axis, designed by Thomas Bonnar in 1822; and on the east by Darnaway Street to the west end of Heriot Row.

McKean

Above: *Jamaica Street*
Below: *St Stephen's Church*

190 INDIA STREET
Planned by **Reid & Sibbald**, built under supervision of **Thomas Bonnar;** work started in 1819.

Mixed development of large flatted blocks and very handsome individual houses marching downhill until it ends in mid air at the road to Stockbridge. Public stairway down through basement areas to North West Circus Place.

191 JAMAICA STREET HOUSING
Philip Cocker and Partners, 1980.

Backland housing association development in honey-coloured rectangular block work; a series of warm, pleasant courtyards of an almshouse quality of restfulness linked to each other by pends.

192 ST. STEPHEN'S CHURCH, St. Vincent Street
William Playfair, 1827.

Octagonal church within a truncated diamond shaped exterior, now divided at gallery level. Its tall tower, with cavernous arched entrance and overscaled detail approached up a huge flight of steps, terminates the view north down Frederick Street and Howe Street with finality.

RCAHMS

Edinburgh Academy

193 ST. BERNARD'S CHURCH, Saxe Coburg
Street, and also **SAXE COBURG PLACE**
James Milne, 1823.

The houses adjoining the church are by
Adam Ogilvie Turnbull, who also revised
Milne's scheme for Saxe Coburg Place,
making the end into a crescent which,
unhappily, was never completed. By now the
New Town classical discipline is becoming
somewhat frayed.

194 EDINBURGH ACADEMY, Henderson Row
William Burn, 1823-36.

Very plain, single storey, Greek Doric essay
of a Calvinist austerity. Domed eliptical hall
within.

St Bernard's Well

195 STOCKBRIDGE PRIMARY SCHOOL,
Hamilton Place
Sir R. Rowand Anderson, 1876.

Gothic after the manner of his master, Sir
George Gilbert Scott.

196 ST. BERNARD'S WELL
Alexander Nasmyth, 1789.

Elegant Doric rotunda on top of a mineral
spring, restored 1888 by Thomas Bonnar.
Statue of Hygeia by D. W. Stevenson 1888.
Forsyth, in 1805, commented that *this spring
has a slight resemblance in flavour to the washings of
a foul gun barrel.*

India Place

197 NEW HOUSING IN STOCKBRIDGE
Michael Laird and Partners: India Place
and Bedford Street: the approach is an urban
one—the former in banks of parallel,
modulated, concrete block tenements; and the
latter, courtyard enclosures of colour-washed
houses with mullioned windows.

G. R. M. Kennedy and Partners: Haugh
Street: white harled, pitched roof,
picturesque, rural-style housing for the
elderly. The nearest Edinburgh has yet

reached to the fashion in other Scots cities of
building *vernacular* fishing village imagery next
to city centres.

Kantel Design: St Bernard's Row:
pedimented block of flats of a pleasing
symmetry, good proportions, and certain
post-modern stylishness.

8 ST. BERNARD CRESCENT/DANUBE STREET/UPPER DEAN STREET
James Milne, 1824.

Redesign of the original scheme with front gardens (as in Ann St.) in favour of a massively urban development, particularly the heavy Greek Doric columned facade on north side of St. Bernard's Crescent. Clearly the feuars considered that a higher return would be gleaned from an apparent extension of the New Town patterns; and instructed the architect to study Playfair accordingly.

St Bernard Crescent

Ann Street

9 ANN STREET
For **Sir Henry Raeburn,**
probably by **James Milne,** 1811.

Ann Street, the first development in this area, consists of facing terraces of different sized houses set at the back of the front garden in reverse of normal pattern. Massing emphasises the quietly old-fashioned rural picturesque, appropriate for its wooded cliffside site, on the country side of the Water of Leith.

0 DEAN BRIDGE
Thomas Telford, 1832.

Above: *Dean Bridge today*

Below: *as planned*

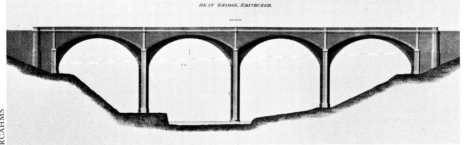

201 LYNEDOCH HOUSE, Lynedoch Place
Roland Wedgwood Associates, 1977.

Pale brick, expressionist block of flats with
chamfered corners and glazed rooftop
conservatory. RIBA Award 1980.

202 DRUMSHEUGH TOLL, Belford Road
Sir George Washington Browne, 1891.

Picturesque Tudorish studio house on cliffside
with red stone turret, designed for artist
Martin Hardie. Originally to have been white
harled in the Arts and Crafts manner with only
the red sandstone details exposed; but a late
decision by the client to abandon the white
harling in favour of stone, radically altered the
building's character.

203 DRUMSHEUGH BATHS, Belford Road
1888 and later by **Sir John J. Burnet.**

Moorish, inside and out, cleverly contrived on
its cliffside. Partially restored by Bamber Gray
& Partners, 1981-82.

Wedgwood

Above: *Lynedoch House* **Below:** *Drumsheugh Toll*

204 BELFORD CHURCH (former), Belford Bridge
Sydney Mitchell, 1889-89.

Gargoyled red sandstone Gothic; Flemish-style
tower becoming octagonal at the top with
spirelet.

205 DRUMSHEUGH GARDENS,
ROTHESAY PLACE and TERRACE,
PALMERSTON PLACE, GROSVENOR
STREET, LANSDOWNE CRESCENT,
GROSVENOR CRESCENT, GLENCAIRN
CRESCENT and EGLINTON CRESCENT.

The part of Edinburgh most resembling the
West End of Victorian Glasgow, extending
particularly to Grosvenor Crescent. Victorian
terraced houses and corner tenements in the
grand style, with great variety in bay-window
details and rhythms, by John Lessels (greater
part of Drumsheugh Gardens, s.e. section
Palmerston Place) Peddie & Kinnear (s.w. side
Drumsheugh Gardens, Rothesay Place,
Palmerston Place Church), Robert Matheson
(Grosvenor Street, Lansdowne Crescent), John
Chesser (greater part of Palmerston Place,
Grosvenor, Glencairn and Eglinton Crescents)
and John Watherston and Sons (Rothesay
Terrace).

McKean

Below: *Drumsheugh Gardens* **Right:** *Rothesay Place*

McKean

McKean

Melville Street and St Mary's Cathedral

206 MELVILLE STREET
Robert Brown. Designed 1814, built 1820-26.

The formal centrepiece of the Western New
Town retaining the repose that George Street
has relinquished. The circus (called the
Crescent) in the middle is by John Lessels,
1855-6, omitting Brown's proposed engaged
porticos: and probably humanising the
composition accordingly. Nos. 2, 3, 7, 9,
have notable interiors by Peddie and
Kinnear. No. 54 Melville Street, further
along, was obstrusively refurbished by Sir
Robert Lorimer as his own house (now Royal
Commission for Ancient and Historic
Monuments, Scotland).

207 ATHOLL CRESCENT
Thomas Bonnar, 1824-25.

Late classical curved crescent, now
undergoing major restoration at east end by
Robert Hurd and Partners. No. 13, the
headquarters of the Saltire Society. Facing
Coates Crescent by Robert Brown, 1813-23.

208 ST. MARY'S CATHEDRAL,
Palmerston Place
Sir George Gilbert Scott, 1873-79.

A sublime, Teutonic visual stop to the end of
Melville Street, Northern early English in
style. The towers were only completed by the
First World War. Interior of considerable
richness, notably stone carving details at
clerestorey level.
Adjacent is **Old East Coates House**, 1615, a
Laird's house, pressed into service, complete
with corbelling and crow-stepped gables.
Adjacent is the Flemish-inspired Song School,
John Oldrid Scott, 1887, with murals by
Phoebe Traquair within, and the **Walpole
Hall,** by Lorimer and Matthew, 1933.

209 HAYMARKET STATION
John Miller, 1840-42.

The oldest Scottish station in anything like its
original state: modest, two-storey, and
vaguely classical with portico. Trainshed
shortly to be moved to Bo'ness.

Melville Street as planned

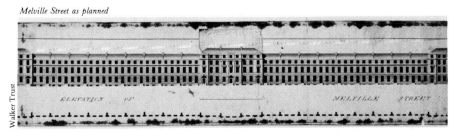

OUTER EDINBURGH

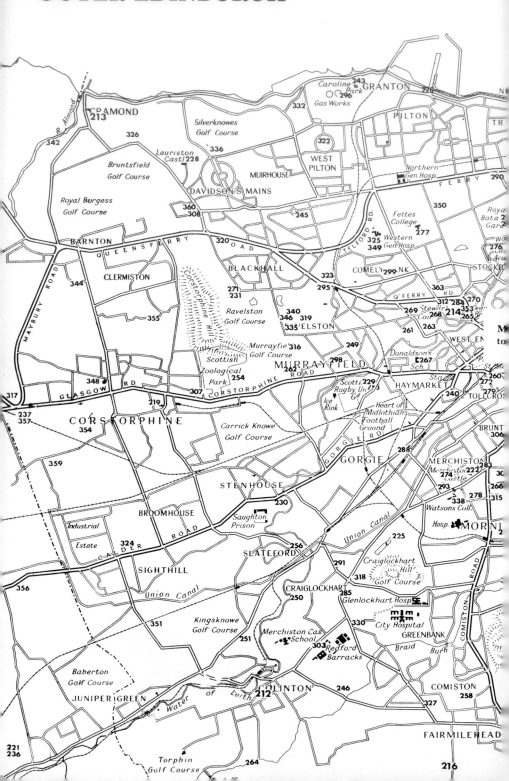

Caroline Park 243
296
332 Gas Works
GRANTON 326
PILTON TR

CRAMOND 213
342 326
Silverknowes
Golf Course
336
322
WEST PILTON
Lauriston Cast/228
Bruntsfield
Golf Course
MUIRHOUSE
Northern
Gen.Hosp.
FERRY 290

Royal Burgess
Golf Course
DAVIDSON'S MAINS
360
308
245
350
Fettes College
277
Roya
Bota 2
Gard

BARNTON
320 OAD
QUEENSFERRY RD
325 Western
349 Gen Hosp
WO
276
Aco
STOCKB

344 CLERMISTON
BLACKHALL
323
295
COMELY 299 NK
363 RD
Q'FERRY
312 284 270
269 Stewart's 268 214 353 Bir
261 263 265 St

Corstorphine Hill
271
231
Ravelston
Golf Course
340
346 319
335 ELSTON
249
WEST EN

355
Murrayfie 316
Golf Course
MURRAYFIELD 267
ROAD
Donaldson's Sch
St Sta
260
272

Scottish
Zoological Park 254
348
307 CORSTORPHINE
RD
Scotti 229
Rugby Un Gd
Ice Rink
Heart of Midlothian
Football Ground
HAYMARKET
240 TOLLCRO
279

317
237
357
GLASGOW RD
219
CORSTORPHINE
354
Carrick Knowe
Golf Course
GORGIE RD
GORGIE
288
BRUNT 306
MERCHISTON
274 Merchiston Castle 222 28
293
338 278 315

359
STENHOUSE
230
266

BROOMHOUSE
Saughton Prison
Union Canal
225
Watsons Coll.
Hosp. MORNI 2

Industrial
Estate
324
ER ROAD
CALDER
256
SLATEFORD
291
Craiglockhart Hill
318 Golf Course

356
SIGHTHILL
Union Canal
CRAIGLOCKHART
250
285
Glenlockhart Hosp
330 City Hospital
GREENBANK

351
Kingsknowe
Golf Course
251
Merchiston Cas School
303 Redford Barracks
Braid Burn
COMISTON RD

Baberton
Golf Course
JUNIPER GREEN
Water of Leith
COLINTON 212
246
COMISTON
327
258

221
236
Torphin
Golf Course
264
FAIRMILEHEAD
216

PORT OF
LEITH

P
Town
Hall
210
o   n
c
d
k
m
l j i
h
e

238

a

Leith Links   g

SEAFIELD

Leith Links

Eastern
Gen. Hosp.

CRAIGENTINNY

Hibernian
Football
Ground   **362**

226   LOCHEND

232

Meadowbank   **221** Restalrig

Calton Hill   **352**   LONDON   RD.

311

PIERSHILL

Swimming
Pool

PORTOBELLO

217   Town
Hall

d a

b

Public Baths

and new
p. 8 & 9.

ley Sta.

Palace of
Holyrood

Jocks
Lodge   **310**

St Anthony's
Chapel

218

YELLOWCRAIG RD.

Figgate
Burn

JOPPA

EASTFIEL

Holyrood Park

Figgate

Meadows

e Meadows

361   **292**   **364**   Dairy

Arthur's Seat
822 ft.

215
DUDDINGSTON

SOUTHFIELD

Bur

Brunstane

239

358 275
343 329

Duddingston Loch

Golf Course

366   **304**   **259**

NEWINGTON

280
GR **314** E

IMONT

Prestonfield
Golf Course   **242**

PRESTONFIELD

345

CRAIGMILLAR

235

NIDDRIE

321

NEWCRA

365

309

313 337

234

328

King's Buildings   **333**
Royal
Observatory   **334**
Quarry   Craigmillar Park
Golf Course

Craigmillar
Castle **220**

INCH

GILMERTON

OLD

DALKEITH

Niddrie Burn

MILLER

raid

Braid Burn

Braid Burn

282   Liberton
Golf
Course

ROAD

Hills
ourse

223

227

LIBERTON

MOREDUN

DANDERHALL

247

Course

Liberton
Hospital   Southfield
Hospital
HYVOTS
BANK

331

GILMERTON

252   **347**
Mortonhall

GRACEMOUNT

ss Margaret Rose
Hospital

44   BURDIEHOUSE

© John Bartholomew & Son Ltd., Edinburgh.

Edinburgh
SECTION TWO

OUTLYING COMMUNITIES

LEITH
NEWHAVEN and GRANTON
CRAMOND
DEAN VILLAGE
DUDDINGSTON
PORTOBELLO
SWANSTON

OUTER EDINBURGH
ARRANGED CHRONOLOGICALLY

A skating party on Duddingston Loch 1844

McKean

Port of Leith in the early 19th Century

INTRODUCTION

The first part of this Guide was arranged on a geographical basis, because the Old Town and the New Town are so compact that they are better described by means of continuous walking routes. The same cannot be said for Edinburgh beyond the New Town, since the administrative area now governed by the City of Edinburgh District Council is so large and diverse. In consequence, this section of the Guide is prepared in two parts: first, a guide to those of Edinburgh's communities which still retain a coherent identity; followed by a chronological guide to those buildings between.

Beyond the Old and the New Town, there are a number of large or small distinct communities. Sandwiched between them and the ever-widening metropolitan centre, were the Castles, Lairds' Houses and Mansions, a surprising number of which still survive. The concentration of such houses around Edinburgh was thought exceptional even three hundred years ago. In 1600, the Duc de Rohan noted that *more than a hundred country-seats are to be found within a radius of two leagues of the town*. Their situation now varies: Dalry House is hemmed in on all sides by Victorian tenements, and Craigentinny House by inter-war housing estates; Craigcrook Castle is still resplendent in its own park; whilst Brunstane House derives its charm partly from its remote isolation.

In modern times, the empty areas between the various communities have been filled up, coincidentally with a major redevelopment of the older inner areas, particularly in central Edinburgh and central Leith. To cater for the housing demands caused by the demolition in the centre, enormous peripheral housing developments were created, first at Niddrie, Craigmillar, and Pilton, and latterly at Muirhouse. The most striking, and possibly strikingly unfortunate, expansion of Edinburgh has been to the south—Gilmerton, Liberton, Oxgangs and Wester Hailes. The passer-by in these districts would be hard put to tell that they were in Edinburgh or, for that matter, in Scotland. One saving grace, however (small though it is), is the architectural coherence and interest of much of the late 1950s productions in the Liberton area: more shallow, green copper roofs, swept porches, spindly balconies and rendered walls. Some of them are quite appealing. East Craigs, and Fairmilehead have been the scene of the comparable expansion in private home ownership. The development of these peripheral areas have coincided—or may indeed have caused—increasing dereliction at the city centre. In the future, the emphasis is likely to be a return to that centre, to fill the gaps, and to repair the damage of the intervening years.

Leith

210 Leith was Edinburgh's port, a *very opulent and flourishing port* in 1669, and a substantial commercial town in its own right, until amalgamation with Edinburgh in 1920. It is situated about the mouth of the Water of Leith and was twice fortified—with a Fort and Citadel, scanty remains of both surviving. The Citadel was built in 1650, and its arched gateway remains (behind wire) in Dock Street. In 1662, John Ray described it as *one of the best fortifications that we ever beheld, passing fair and sumptuous. Three forts . . . two platforms . . . works round about faced with freestone . . . a good capacious chapel . . . the Piazza within as large as Trinity College (in Cambridge) Great Court.* Although grossly neglected in recent years, and having lost many of its finer buildings—including the Renaissance Tolbooth, Leith is currently undergoing a revival and refurbishment with the help of the Scottish Development Agency.

As well as the docks and old waterfront (the Shore) there is a real urban centre in Bernard Street and a splendid park in Leith Links. The architectural character of the town stems from the juxtaposition of big warehouses and very smart prettily detailed, later-Georgian houses and public buildings. It has also two major Scottish Greek Revival buildings.

RCAHMS

Leith Citadel Gateway in 1910

a LEITH WALK

Grand parade between Edinburgh and Leith, the northern end being founded upon old fortifications. Note particularly **Smith's Place,** premises of Messrs Raimes Clark, 1812, with fine fan-light; and Pilrig-Dalmeny Church, chunky Teulonesque Gothic with spire by Peddie & Kinnear 1860-62.

b SOUTH LEITH CHURCH and GRAVEYARD, Kirkgate

Remains of a fine 15th century church inside Thomas Hamilton's 1848 indifferent Gothic replacement. Hamilton was a great Greek, but an indifferent Goth. 17/19th century monuments and rows of Gothic burial enclosures.

McKean

Smith Place

c TRINITY HOUSE, Kirkgate
Thomas Brown, 1816.

A rather provincial, fat-columned and pedimented building with an undisturbed interior. Charitable foundation for merchant seamen.

d ST. MARY STAR OF THE SEA ROMAN CATHOLIC CHURCH, Constitution Street
E. W. Pugin and J. A. Hansom, 1854.

Severe, peculiar and blackened church. North aisle 1900, re-orientation and new apse 1910.

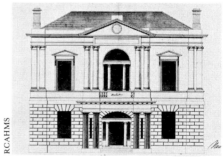

RCAHMS

Trinity House

Leith Exchange

*e OLD LEITH TOWN HALL
and POLICE STATION,* Constitution Street
R. & R. Dickson, 1828.

Quality neo-classical job, with one style to
Constitution Street and a very different one to
Queen Charlotte Street. Notable interior
enlarged and enriched by James Simpson of
Leith 1891.
Elegant late Georgian merchants' houses in
both these streets.

f CLAREMONT PARK, The Links
From 1827.

Laid out by Thomas Hamilton who probably
designed No. 5, 6 and 7.

Above: *Leith Bank* **Below:** *Corn Exchange*

g SEAFIELD BATHS (formerly),
1-3 Seafield Place and 2-4 Seafield Road
John Paterson, 1813.

Neglected, isolated neo-classical corner, with
single-storey Doric porticos, and domed
rotunda corner, Would look spectacular if
cleaned.

h LEITH EXCHANGE BUILDING
Thomas Brown, 1809.

Incorporates the 1783 Assembly Rooms in
Assembly Street. The pedimented facade to
Constitution Street is grand even by
Edinburgh standards, designed in a style
that, in the New Town, would be thought to
be concealing terraced houses.

i FORMER LEITH BANK (now Royal Bank
of Scotland), Bernard Street
1804.

Probably by John Paterson (pupil of Robert
Adam), similar in a miniature way, to his
demolished Montgomerie House, Ayrshire.
Bowed front with Ionic columns and dome.
Reputed to contain painted-out ceiling murals
of some joy. Symmetrical flanking tenements
1807-15.

Customs House

j **KING'S WARK,** Bernard Street and Shore
Early 18th century.

Harled with a Scots chimney gable, with a
fine doorway and a pub in the ground floor.
Restored by Robert Hurd & Partners, 1975.

k **SIGNAL TOWER,** north end of the Shore
Robert Mylne, 1685.

Originally a windmill: battlements later.

l **ANDRO LAMB'S HOUSE,** Water's Close,
the Shore
Early 17th century.

Above: *Andro Lamb's House* **Below:** *St. Ninian's
Manse*

Gables galore, with roundels, corbels, and a
steep pitched roof. Scots-Hanseatic pattern
with warehousing above and below the
merchant's house. Rescued in 1939 and
restored 1960 by Robert Hurd and Partners
as old People's day centre. Property of the
National Trust for Scotland.

m **CUSTOMS HOUSE,** Commercial Street
Robert Reid, 1812.

Magisterial Greek Doric building, showing
Reid at his most effective. The outside and
inside stairs are by William Burn, 1824.

n **ST. NINIAN'S MANSE,** Quayside Street
Late 16th century: subsequently altered.

Three storey L-shaped building with
somewhat crumbled crow-stepped gables, still
observable in later mutation to granary and
mill. The staircase is capped by a striking,
ogival-headed timber turret of 17th century,
similar to that originally capping the spire of
the Tron Kirk, High Street, and the north
tower of the Chapel Royal at Holyrood before
its collapse in 18th century.

o NORTH LEITH PARISH CHURCH,
Madeira Street
William Burn, 1813.

Burn's earliest major work in Edinburgh:
Greek Doric portico and classical steeple
evidently based on work by the Glasgow
architect David Hamilton. Unusual plan with
pulpit at entrance end. Restored 1950 by Ian
G. Lindsay.

p HOUSING, Portland Street/Lindsay Road
City of Edinburgh Architects' Department,
1978.

Extensive housing redevelopment, bounded
on one side by the wall of the old Leith Fort,
and overshadowed by the competition
winning towers of the Leith Fort development
(Shaw Stewart and Perry, 1963). A fine
contrast. The upper reaches consist of white-
harled pitched roof terraced houses facing
courtyards, of a distinctly seaside character.
The blocks of flats facing the main road are
grander, like Hanseatic warehouses, with
two-storey pitched roofs, lacks the odd hoist
and hayloft. Well worth comparing to the
new SSHA housing development in Bowling
Green St (1981), the barrier block of which
has a strongly modelled blockwork facade.

Portland Street housing: Leith Fort behind

11 Newhaven and Granton

Old seaport village celebrated for its fishwives
where the Great Michael, the largest vessel of
its time, was built in 1511 (some timbers from
the Great Michael are thought to have been
built into Gladstone's Land.) The harbour is
still used by fishing and pleasure boats.
Fishmarket Square and streets of red
pantiled, exterior-staired houses were
comprehensively restored, rebuilt or in-filled
by Ian G Lindsay & Partners.

ANNFIELD, Newhaven
Basil Spence, 1959.

Small, stepped, terraced houses, a variation
on those earlier completed by Spence at
Dunbar harbour: external staircases, spindly
details, and a variety of colours.

Above: *Wester Close, Newhaven* **Below:** *Annfield*

BOSWELL ROAD, Trinity

Terrace of fine sea captains' houses possibly
influenced by Thomas Hamilton, the
northern-facing profile reminiscent of
Vanbrugh's Northumberland mansion of Seaton
Delaval. Good ironwork.
Trinity became a favourite district for wildly
varying 19th century villas, notably in
Lennox Row and York Road.

GRANTON SQUARE

Two facing commercial Italianate blocks by
William Burn 1838, associated with the Duke
of Buccleuch's harbour development. Some
simple artisan housing by the same architect
to the east, together with some later houses by
John Hawkins, 1848.

212 *Colinton*

Shona Adam

Rustic Cottages

Mill village in the steep valley of Water of Leith, with suburban villas clearly laid out to an English, Home Counties, ideal. Church 1771 on earlier foundation, reconstructed by Sydney Mitchell 1907 with neo-Byzantine interior. Adjoining Manse 1783. Became railway suburb, and perhaps as a result, notable for series of villas by Sir Robert Lorimer, Sir Rowand Anderson and other architects of note.

COLINTON CASTLE
16-17th century.

L-plan tower long a romantic ruin in the grounds of Merchiston Castle School, Colinton Road (1923 by W. J. Walker Todd). Ruinous 17th century dovecot adjacent. Note also **Colinton House,** the distinguished Georgian mansion of Sir William Forbes of Pitsligo, 1801, (designed by Richard Crichton

but probably adapting a scheme commission from Thomas Harrison), now adapted for school use. Forbes was a noted banker, one of those who financed the New Town developments.

SPYLAW, Bridge Road, Colinton
Rear part 1650, north front added 1773.

Pedimented centrepiece and pleasant balcony. Home of James Gillespie, snuff merchant who founded school. Note his burial place in Colinton Churchyard.

SIR WILLIAM FRASER HOMES,
52 Spylaw Bank Road, Colinton
A. F. Balfour Paul.

Almshouse square in Scots 17th century manner: an excellent catalogue of traditional details, beautifully put together, and wholly incongruous in this English style suburb.

1-7 RUSTIC COTTAGES, Colinton Road
Sir Robert Lorimer, 1901.

Pleasant white walled and slated cottages with peculiar dormer windows. The adjacent **St. Cuthbert's,** Westgarth Avenue, a good, rather High, Episcopal Church by Rowand Anderson 1887-97, with yet another variation on the old Tron Kirk steeple.
There are many Lorimer developments in Colinton, including Laverockdale House (1914), 3 Spylaw Avenue (1897), 19 Spylaw Park (1899), 47 Spylaw Bank Road and 1 Pentland Road (1914). 14, 21, 26 and 32 Gillespie Road are also by Lorimer (1895-8). Lorimer used to refer to his *Colinton manner,*—implying long, low villas, usually white harled, with steep roofs and monumental chimney stacks. Later he itched to get to something larger, dismissing his Colinton achievements as: *starved, whitewashed houses.*

A Lorimer "Colinton Cottage"

National Monuments Record

MISS GVTHRIE-WRIGHT'S

13 Cramond

Remains of an industrial village based on ironworks by the mouth of River Almond, largely 1790. Cottages restored 1961 by Ian Lindsay & Partners. Tall and narrow Cramond Tower, 15th century, built by Bishops of Dunkeld, recently restored, has a fine doorway and an unusual plan indicating that it might once have formed one tower of a larger castle or palace. It stands in the grounds of nearby Cramond House (18th century). Interesting, partially excavated remains of a Roman settlement beside 17th century Kirk with 15th century tower. Old Cramond Brig, upstream, early 16th century, Harbour used by pleasure boats; Tidal causeway to island; a good Inn.

Below: *Cramond Tower* Below left: *Cramond Kirk*

14 Dean Village (Water of Leith Village)

Historic meal-mill village in chasm at edge of New Town, whose *pungent tanneries and its blacksmith's shop melodious with the clank of the anvil,* a visitor noted in 1910. Its purpose is past, and few mill buildings survive. Note particularly **West Mill** (1805) nicely restored as 22 flats by Philip Cocker and Partners in 1973, and **Stewart's Coach House,** Bell's Brae by Thomas Moncur, 1881, restored by Robert Matthew Johnson-Marshall & Partners for their own offices.

Left: *Stewart's Coach House* Below: *West Mill*

F

McKean

Above: *Water of Leith Village in 1693. The Baxter's Granary is the large building in the centre* **Left:** *Hawthorn buildings* **Bottom:** *Well Court Hall*

Cocker

BAXTER'S GRANARY, Bells Brae 1675.

Large steep roofed barn with two projecting stair towers, one with heraldic panel and motto, restored as flats 1974 by F. R. Stevenson.

WELL COURT
Sydney Mitchell & Wilson, 1884.

17th century Scots fantasy for John Ritchie Findlay, philanthropic owner of **The Scotsman,** designed to be seen from his house in Rothesay Terrace. Flats, social hall and clock tower; the hall now an architect's office. Note particularly the clock tower: undoubtedly modelled on the old Tron Kirk steeple, albeit smaller in scale.

HAWTHORN BUILDINGS
Dunn and Findlay, 1895.

Pleasant yellow-ochre half timbered row of pitched roofed buildings, restored by Philip Cocker and Partners. Findlay was John Ritchie Findlay's son.

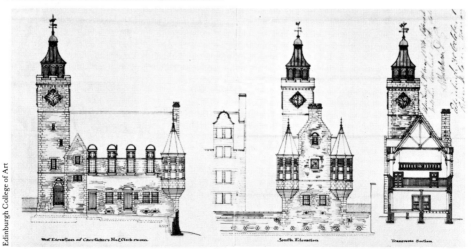

Edinburgh College of Art

15 Duddingston

Compact, formerly weaving, settlement in lee of Arthur's Seat; facing Duddingston Loch. Handsome houses in Old Church Lane and the Causeway.

DUDDINGSTON CHURCH

12th century, in 17-18th century disguise, partly restored by Rowand Anderson. Romanesque doorway and chancel arch: north Aisle dated 1631. Early 19th century watch-tower, by Robert Brown. Louping-on-Stane outside.

DUDDINGSTON HOUSE, Milton Road Sir William Chambers, 1768.

One of the finest 18th century houses in Britain, with typical Chambers austerity. Simple villa form, with Corinthian temple portico. No basement. Built with few domestic facilities, the service and stables placed in the superb quadrangle adjacent. Surrounding park by James Robertson includes a Doric Temple by Chambers. Now the Mansion House Hotel and Motel.

Above: *The Village.* Below: *The Church* Below left: *Duddingston House*

6 Swanston (Pentland Hills)

18th century community of whitewashed rubble cottages, restored by the City in 1962 and displaying the only surviving thatched roofs in Lothian. Note no. 16 (Schoolhouse), and Swanston Cottage (1761) once summer home of Robert Louis Stevenson

217 *Portobello*

Portobello was to Edinburgh what Brighton and Hove were to London, without the Prince Regent and his pavilion. It thus contains a large quantity of fine buildings produced in the 150 years during which it was a fashionable place to live. No stucco here, of course: just pleasant regency villas of a seaside type. Unfortunately, fashion is in retreat, and the town is suffering.

It started in the mid 18th century with a thatch cottage of that name (after the naval victory of 1739) on the east coast road. A builder and brickmaker, William Jamieson, bought 40 acres in 1763 and built villas of which only one now survives—the curious Portobello Tower at the west end of the Prom, incorporating medieval and later stone fragments taken from buildings demolished in Edinburgh's High Street, in its red brick walls.

Sea bathing began c. 1790, the road became the High Street, and successive Georgian developments covered these small estates: starting in 1801 with Bath Street which now combines all the four elements of Portobello; elegant Georgian houses, spectacular Victorian tenements (e.g. Edward Calvert's Brighton and Windsor Mansions of 1899), 1930s swank (e.g. Bowhill Gibson's cinema of 1938, now altered) and recent gimcrack. Joppa, immediately to the east, grew more slowly and is much more sedate—pretty Georgian and solid Victorian housing looking at each other suspiciously.

I Fisher

Portobello Tower

a **OLD PARISH CHURCH,** Bellfield Street **William Sibbald,** 1809, the domed clocktower added in 1839.
Hall by **Alan Reiach and Partners,** 1964.

Pleasant, small, classical church, in an area of comparable character.

b **ST. JOHN'S ROMAN CATHOLIC CHURCH,** Brighton Place **J. T. Walford,** 1903.

Gothic, with an idiosyncratic, Art-Nouveau influenced steeple like five blunt pencils, clearly visible as a landmark from the railway. Brighton Place and Rosefield (called after Jamieson's own villa) were developed by the architect John Baxter in the 1820s. Brighton Crescent, behind the church, is particularly nice: semi-detached villas more akin to contemporary London developments —e.g. the Paragon in Blackheath.

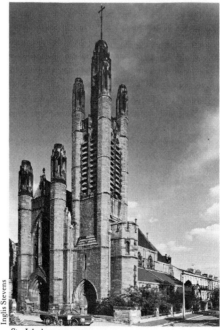

Inglis Stevens

St. John's

Police Station

Regent Street

c **POLICE STATION** (former Town Hall),
High Street
Robert Paterson, 1877.

Crammed with turrets and crowned with iron
cresting.

d **REGENT STREET**

Full of choice villas laid out in 1815 by Lewis
A. Wallace together with Marlborough Street
and Straiton Place. More villas in Windsor
Place, including the grand Windsor Place
Lodge and the Gothic No. 15.

e **SWIMMING POOL,** Portobello Promenade
W. A. Macartney, City Engineer, 1934-7.

The pool retains considerable *moderne*
stylishness—particularly the three tier diving
board. Now disused, although worth saving.
Contained early wave machine.

f **BRIDGE STREET/PIPE STREET**
City Architects' Department, 1979-82.

Pleasant but dense development of one and
two storey houses in light brown brick and
brown tiles. The houses are grouped around
courtyards, and exemplify the trend toward a
humanist scale, eschewing anything overtly
architectural. Massive, brick bottle-kilns
survive nearby.

Pipe Street

Medieval Period

218 ST. MARGARET'S WELL, Holyrood Park
15th century.

A small gem, moved from Meadowbank: rib-
vaulted well-house set into the hillside, fed by
a natural spring.

219 CORSTORPHINE CHURCH
Early 15th century.

A fine specimen of a medieval, Scots,
collegiate kirk, dominated by its heavy west
tower, stone spire, and a roof of great stone
slabs (now concrete). Good tracery, and
notable monuments inside and outside.
Interior largely restored by George
Henderson. Note the nearby **Dower House,**
High Street, of 1660: and the circular 16th
century dovecot in Dovecot Road containing
more than 1000 pigeon holes, a relic of
Corstorphine Castle.

220 CRAIGMILLAR CASTLE
14-16th century.

L-plan tower with stone vaulted great hall,
enclosed by two fortified ranges of outer
buildings, one with round corner towers and
machicolations. Includes ruins of a chapel, a
Dovecot, and a Rose garden. Roofless but
remarkably complete; one of Scotland's most
impressive medieval remains. **Ancient
Monument open to visitors. Guide Book
available.**

221 LENNOX TOWER, Currie
15th century.

Much ruined tower with thick walls standing
in enclosure some of which survives.

222 MERCHISTON TOWER, Colinton Road
15th century.

L-plan tower, formerly home of John Napier,
discoverer of logarithms, carefully restored by
City Architects' Department and now
embalmed within Napier College (by Alison
& Hutchison 1964). Contains 1581 painted
ceiling removed from Prestongrange, East
Lothian and its own 17th century plaster
ceiling. The early 19th century stone gateway
was assembled from older pieces.
Napier College is designed around two open
quadrangles, and caters for over 4000
students.

223 LIBERTON TOWER, Liberton
15th century.

Four square, four storeys, uncompromising
fortress with stone-slabbed roof and stone
vaults. Surrounded by 1701 farm steading.

St. Margaret's Well

224 RESTALRIG CHURCH
and ST. TRIDUANA'S AISLE
15th century.

The aisle (known as St. Triduana's Well)
restored by Thomas Ross, is a 15th century
vaulted hexagon 35 feet across, with central
pier. Originally capped by a further chamber
above.
This great church, originally the principal
church for Leith, attracted in 1580 the
attention of the Kirk Assembly who resolved
that *the Kirk of Restalrig, as a Monument of
Idolatrie, be raysit and utterlie cast downe and
destroyed.* Only scant remains of the Choir
survived for William Burn to build upon in
1838. **Ancient Monument open to visitors.**
Enclosing wall survives from a former Priory.
Note also 62 Restalrig Road South with
moulded doorway (1678).

Above: *Craigmillar Castle: The great hall in 1846, drawn by R W Billings* **Below:** *the Castle from the air*

Corstorphine Church

Above: *Liberton Tower* **Below:** *Merchiston Tower*

St. Triduana's Well as drawn for restoration by Dr Thomas Ross (from EAA Transactions)

16th Century

225 CRAIG HOUSE, Royal Edinburgh Hospital for Mental Disorders, Craighouse Road 1565.

Much be-gabled Laird's house with crowsteps and stair-tower, extended in 18th century. The neighbouring Craighouse Asylum (Thomas Clouston Clinic) is a vast château with châtelet dependencies by Sydney Mitchell, 1893.

226 LOCHEND CASTLE, Marionville Road

A 16th century fragment with a massive chimney, adjoining the early 19th century mansion which overlooks the Loch. Circular 16th century dovecot.

227 LIBERTON HOUSE, Liberton Drive Late 16th century.

L-plan mansion enlarged 1675 and picturesquely restored in the 20th century by Sir William Kininmonth and Sir Basil Spence.

228 LAURISTON CASTLE, Cramond Road North Late 16th century.

Tall T-shaped tower with turrets built by Sir Archibald Napier, and greatly extended 1824 by William Burn in grand neo-Jacobean manner. Once the home of Scots financier to Louis XIV, John Law. Splendidly furnished Edwardian interior. Latin-inscribed armorial panel states: *I do not acknowledge the stars as either the rulers of life or the causes of my good fortune. The things which I possess I ascribe to the goodness of God.* **Edinburgh District Council: open to visitors. Guide book available.** Croquet in the gardens overlooking the Forth, and tea in the adjoining farm steading.

229 ROSEBURN HOUSE, Roseburn Avenue 1582.

Small, harled, tower, later extended to

McKean

Lauriston Castle

courtyard, only half of which now survives. Formerly overlooking the Water of Leith, now overlooked by Murrayfield.

230 STENHOUSE MANSION, Stenhouse Mill Lane North wing mid 16th century, majority 1623.

Pleasantly primitive building of steep roofs and tall chimney stalks, restored 1962 by Ian G. Lindsay as conservation centre, now run by Ancient Monuments Division of SDD. **Property of the National Trust for Scotland.**

Stenhouse

Ian G Lindsay

Craigcrook Castle, with Corstorphine Hill behind.

Alison Hutchinson

1 CRAIGCROOK CASTLE, Craigcrook Road
16th century Z-plan, extended 1835 by
William Playfair.

Romantic baronial mansion in its original
landscaped grounds and rural atmosphere.
Murals by David Roberts. Had been a
lunatic asylum but was most famous as the
country retreat of Francis Jeffrey, Lord
Advocate and editor of the **Edinburgh
Review.** William Cobbett thought it a *very
delightful little country house* in 1832. Converted
by Alison & Hutchinson into architects'
offices, 1968, with the addition of a single-
storey, glazed pavilion on a stone
plinth in the stable area.

Craigentinny Mausoleum in the 1880s

RIAS Collection

232 CRAIGENTINNY HOUSE, Loaning Road
16th century.

Striking, heavily turreted tower-house
mouldering in the midst of council estate.
Altered 1849 by David Rhind, much enlarged
and since reduced again. Note also the
Craigentinny Mausoleum in nearby
Craigentinny Crescent, 1848 by David
Rhind, with sculpture by Alfred Gatley.

Craigentinny House

McKean

17th Century

RCAHMS

Bruntsfield House, before conversion to school

233 BRUNTSFIELD HOUSE, Bruntsfield Place 1605.

Z-plan, three storeys, with stair turrets and crowstep gables. Restored and reduced to its original size as part of James Gillespie's High School by Rowand Anderson, Kininmonth and Paul, 1964.

234 THE INCH, Old Dalkeith Road

1617 (on the basis of earlier building, traces of which survive internally).
Crowstepped, three storey L-plan mansion originally approached over a drawbridge, with ogee roofed stair tower. The later two storey extension with vigorously carved dormers, forms a courtyard. Some similarities to Gogar House. Late Georgian addition heavily remodelled 1891 by MacGibbon and Ross. Grounds are a public park. A splendid mansion of great history, now suffering badly as a Community Centre. Edinburgh is not very good with its stately homes: Pilrig, Niddrie Marischal and Saughton Hall were all burnt out. It would be tragic if that happened to The Inch.

235 PEFFERMILL HOUSE, Peffermill Road 1636, possibly by **William Aytoun,** built for **Edward Edgar.**

Three storey L-plan house restored and recreated internally 1981 by Nicholas Groves-Raines as his house and office. Austere, harled, steep roofed building, with fine armorial panel, string courses and dormers. Thought to be Sir Walter Scott's model for Dumbiedykes in **Heart of Midlothian.**

236 BABERTON HOUSE, Currie
Sir James Murray, 1622-3.

Consists of a main block with projecting wings—an increasingly typical Scots plan once defensiveness lost importance. Originally circular stair towers in re-entrants. Courtyard filled, 1765, with octagonal, five-storey bay. Good interiors and dormers.

McKean

Above: *The Inch from the rear*
Below: *Peffermill House*

Groves-Raines

Brunstane House

McKean

37 GOGAR HOUSE
1626

Tall, L-plan mansion, semi-octagonal staircase inside the L, circular one at the heel. Fine array of turrets and dormers. Semi-octagonal staircase corbelled out into a square one, topped by a balustrade. Aircraft.

38 PILRIG HOUSE, Pilrig
1638, remodelled late 17th century.

Barely 20 years ago, a delightful country mansion, L-shaped, raised first floor, with fine decorative gable. Now a derelict shell in a public open space: burnt by vandals after being *mothballed* by the City, pending a new use.

39 BRUNSTANE HOUSE, Brunstane Road North (off Milton Road)
1639.

An important house, with 16th century origins, sporting projecting corner stair towers with ogee and conical roofs, and containing outstanding interiors. Largely rebuilt 1639 as L-plan, and later extended to U-plan by Sir William Bruce for the Duke of Lauderdale at the same time as the pair were refashioning Thirlestane Castle, Lauder. *I will only patch what is already built* wrote Lauderdale to Bruce *and make myself a very convenient lodge, but will by no means build a fine house there.* The Lodge Lauderdale proposed contained only four drawing rooms, three major bed chambers, a great chamber, a great staircase, a dining room for the gentlewoman, another for the steward and waiters, another for the meanest servants to eat in, a room for tobacco, a room for sweetmeats, a room for candlesticks and brooms, a buttery, kitchens, closets, and cellars; and *my beloved little low gallery . . . where I will have a billiard board and other*

conveniences. Later considerably rebuilt and remodelled by William Adam, with outstanding plasterwork.

240 DALRY HOUSE, Orwell Place
Mid 17th century.

Country house of the Chieslie family overwhelmed by tenements. White harled block with two, projecting semi-hexagonal towers with ogee roofs: good interior plasterwork. Restored 1963 as old people's day centre by Robert Hurd & Partners.

Shona Adam

Dalry House

241 WHITEHOUSE, Whitehouse Loan
1670.

Four storeyed building. Adjacent St.
Margaret's Convent, has square, ogee roofed
entrance tower to the convent by Gillespie
Graham, 1835; his Norman Gothic Chapel
has a late Gothic chancel addition of 1896 by
Archibald McPherson.

242 PRESTONFIELD HOUSE,
Prestonfield Road
1687, probably by **Robert Mylne.**

One of Edinburgh's prettiest houses in an
incomparable location adjoining the Queen's
Park. Replacement for a house destroyed by
fire in 1681 riot, the exterior is white harled
with golden stone dressings, capped by twin,
shaped gables. Front porte-cochère, and
ballroom to rear, added in 1818 when the
court between the two wings was filled in.
Rich interiors, one with leather hangings.
Stables circular in plan, 1816, now roofless
and setting for a semi-permanent marquee.
Peacocks. Now an hotel.

243 CAROLINE PARK, Shore Road, Granton
Possibly by **Robert Mylne with James
Smith,** mainly 1685-1696.

Splendid quadrangular mansion of Lord
Tarbat, (previously Sir George *bluidy*
Mackenzie), around an earlier house, with an
imposing entrance front with centrepiece and
ogee roofed towers. Shaped gables to rear.
Fine ceilings, panelling, staircase and corner
fireplaces. An inscribed stone by Tarbat
above the door refers to the house as a *cottage.*
Adjacent 17th century dovecot and gates sole
survivors of 16th century Granton Castle.
Revolting environment.

Above: *Prestonfield House, note the peacocks*
Below: *Caroline Park: note the gasholders*

18th Century

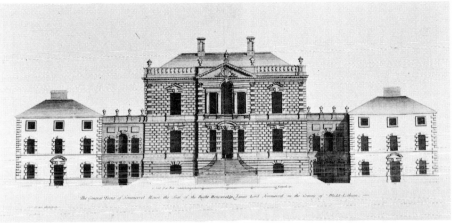

RCAHMS

William Adam's drawing for Somerville House (The Drum) from Vitruvius Scoticus

44 MORTON HOUSE, 19 Winton Loan 1702.

Plain house remodelled c. 1800 with the characteristics of a late Georgian villa. Rubble belvedere, as imitation tower house with circular angle tower, in grounds. Symmetrical gateway and pavilions on approach axis.

45 DRYLAW HOUSE, Groathill Road North 1718

Two-storey and basement mansion with tall chimneys and a swept roof, not dissimiliar to the plainer mansions of Sir William Bruce. The east front was remodelled with pedimented frontispiece in the late 18th century. Good original interiors, restored by Peter Julien. Lectern dovecot nearby.

RCAHMS

Drylaw House

46 REDFORD HOUSE, Redford Road 18th-19th century.

Large, two storey, harled, U-plan house, with sculpture niches and decorative internal plasterwork. The **Drummond Scrolls** by the entrance is a lodge constructed of carved features from William Adam's demolished Royal Infirmary (1738). The scale of the Infirmary may be imagined from the fact that this house is effectively the centre part of the attic storey of the original building.

Drummond Scrolls, Redford House

47 DRUM HOUSE, Gilmerton 1726-34 by **William Adam.**

Otherwise known as Somerville House. Originally planned as a central pavilion with two wings, the eastern wing never built. As finished, the house has three bays, with a central pediment, and the usual urned and balustraded parapet. A fine curving staircase leads up to the main entrance. Has something of Adam's frequently vulgar exuberance. Fine later plasterwork by Calderwood & Clayton.

McKean

248 EAST MORNINGSIDE HOUSE,
Clinton Road
1726 onwards.

Two storeyed house with pitched, dormered
roof: harled with stone dressings. Once home
of novelist Susan Ferrier.

249 MURRAYFIELD HOUSE,
Murrayfield Avenue
1735.

Early Georgian Laird's house transformed by
Baroque doorway, and pediment
surmounting second floor Venetian window.
Harled.

250 REDHALL HOUSE,
Craiglockhart Drive South
James Robertson, 1758.

A nice, rural Laird's mansion with rusticated
bay windows, pediment and urns, with
Edwardian alterations in style. New houses
for **Redhall Bank Children's Centre** by
Lothian Region Architects 1980, pleasantly
and plainly designed in warm brick with neat
roofs. Behind can be found English style,
expensive suburb, Otterburn Park.

251 HAILES HOUSE, Hailes Avenue
Sir James Clerk, 1767.

Plain mansion with unusual details, odd
decoration, and an Edwardianised roof. Now
beached as an hotel amidst a 1930's district of
houses with sunburst doors.

252 MORTONHALL HOUSE, Mortonhall Road
John Baxter, 1769.

Imposing building, in fine setting behind the
Braid Hills, nearly square in plan,
pedimented back and front with an added
Doric porch. Partly late 18th century
interiors.

253 INVERLEITH HOUSE,
Royal Botanical Gardens
David Henderson, 1774.

Plain, douce Laird's mansion with eliptical
bow for staircase over entrance, and obliquely
sited pavilions. Still (1982) the Scottish
National Gallery of Modern Art, with Henry
Moores in the garden, and Barbara
Hepworths neaby, functioning as a climbing
frame for young visitors.

254 BEECHWOOD, Corstorphine Road
1780.

Foursquare mansion high on the hillside
beside the zoo, enhanced by later bow-ended
wings, with large windows. Some good
ceilings.

255 HERMITAGE OF BRAID, off Braid Road
1785. Possibly by **Robert Burn.**

Heavy, castellated house with Gothic
Venetian windows set into the hillside.
Adjacent ice-house of interest.

RCAHMS

Mortonhall

AIC

Inverleith House with sculpture

Scott Robertson

Hermitage of Braid

19th Century

6 UNION CANAL AQUEDUCTS at Slateford, Lanark Road

The first, 1818, is by Hugh Baird, and the second is a reinforced concrete design of 1937. Adjacent, fourteen-arched rail viaduct is by John Miller, 1838.

7 INVERLEITH ROW, HOWARD PLACE and WARRISTON CRESCENT

Early examples of terraced and semi-detached villas and houses in what was then suburbia. Howard Place by Gillespie Graham 1809, is a two-storey and basement row with front gardens; Warriston Crescent, 1818, is similar without the basement areas and rustication omitted; Inverleith Row has pretentious classical villas planned by Thomas Brown 1823 overlooking the Arboretum. No. 8, recently restored by Ian G. Lindsay and Partners, is by William Playfair who was probably also responsible for several others of similar but less grand design.

8 COMISTON HOUSE, Camus Avenue 1815.

Unspectacular, small country mansion with pedimented facade with giant pilasters and elegant fanlight. Now an hotel. 16th century dovecot nearby.

9 BLACKET PLACE
James Gillespie Graham, laid out 1825, completed 1860.

Select suburban estate of small detached and semi-detached classical villas, with a *rus in urbe* layout. Supervised by lodges whose gates were closed at night, Bloomsbury style. The most distinguished house is Arthur Lodge (see below).

Arthur Lodge

RCAHMS

Blacket Place

ARTHUR LODGE, 60 Dalkeith Road 1830, probably by **Thomas Hamilton.**

Grecian Villa of great originality with central atrium stairwell, and later eccentric stair banisters of solid Ionic columns. Some remarkable affinities to Alexander Thomson's (Alexander *Greek* Thomson was Glasgow's greatest mid-Victorian architect) villas in Glasgow: e.g. incised stone carving; glazing directly into stone; disposition of the wings, and internal design of bays.

260 GARDNER'S CRESCENT and
85-115 MORRISON STREET
R. & R. Dickson, 1826.

Clever curving terrace with orderless pilasters, whose window glazing bars line up with the joints in the stonework: more the kind of liberties Glasgow took with classical architecture than we are accustomed to find in Edinburgh.

Joe Rock

McKean

John Watson's

261 JOHN WATSON'S SCHOOL, Belford Road
William Burn, 1828.

Long, very plain two storey frontage
energised by strongly projecting central
Greek Doric portico, and marginally modified
by two shallow end pavilions. To be the new
Scottish National Gallery of Modern Art.

262 BELMONT, Ellersly Road
W. H. Playfair, 1828.

Grand Italianate villa, with bold porte-
cochère and notable Grecian interior: already
early Victorian in character whilst Playfair's
pure classicism was to survive elsewhere for
quite a time.

263 DEAN EDUCATION CENTRE, Belford
Road
Thomas Hamilton, 1833, as the Dean
Orphanage.

Dry Revival of English Baroque, the end
towers derived from Thomas Archer
(St. John's Church in Smith Square, London)
Vanbrugh (Kings Weston, Bristol) and
drawings by George Dance.

264 BONALY TOWER, Bonaly Road
William Playfair, 1836.

Crisp Scots tower house grafted on to existing
farmhouse for Lord Cockburn, with a lavish
library wing later added by Sydney Mitchell,
1888. Now divided.
Unless some avenging angel expel me wrote
Cockburn *I shall never leave that paradise.
Everything except the two burns, the few old trees
and the mountains are my own work and to a great
extent the work of my own hands. Human nature is
incapable of enjoying more happiness than has been
my lot here.*

265 HOLY TRINITY CHURCH, Dean Bridge
John Henderson, 1838.

Terraced crypt modelled on St. John's Princes
Street; church itself based on a Charles Barry
prototype. Style may be codified as
picturesquely weak perpendicular. Preserved as an
electricity sub station.

266 1 CHURCHILL
John Henderson, 1842.

Good example of early middle-class
Edinburgh suburban villas; symmetrical, two
storey, classical proportions and portico.
More rural and less pretentious than
Inverleith Row.

Dean Education Centre

Joe Rock

Donaldson's School: Playfair's original elevation

7 DONALDSON'S SCHOOL,
Haymarket Terrace
W. H. Playfair, 1842-54.

A school for the deaf, based on English Tudor and Jacobean Mansions. Quadrangular, with square towers, octagonal turrets, buttresses, chimneys, tall windows, and large chapel on north.

8 DEAN CEMETRY
David Cousin, 1845.

Edinburgh's richest collection of memorials, including those by Playfair for himself, Rutherford and Jeffrey on the west wall: also original carved stones from demolished mansion house of Dean which this cemetery displaced.

9 DANIEL STEWART'S COLLEGE,
Queensferry Road
David Rhind, 1849-55.

Grand, turreted school, blending the influence of George Heriot's and the Scots Renaissance, with English Jacobean in a

Daniel Stewart's

formal terraced garden setting. The former chapel is now a library, and the courtyard has been roofed as a hall. Now within grounds **DEAN PARK BOARDING HOUSE,** amazing bow-fronted Second Empire mansion by F. T. Pilkington 1874.

270 CLARENDON CRESCENT, ETON TERRACE, OXFORD TERRACE
John Tait, 1850-53

Terraces just north of Dean Bridge still retaining some traces of New Town classical, but the early stages of the metamorphosis to Victorian are clearly visible.

271 75 CRAIGCROOK ROAD
Mid 19th century.

Cottage ornée, Shropshire style. Rough yellow plaster, rustic timber work, and lozenge-shaped windows. No architect known, but possibly by Playfair who turned out the occasional rustic exercise elsewhere, and was working only a few yards away in Craigcrook Castle.

272 ROSEBANK COTTAGES,
Gardner's Crescent
**Alexander MacGregor
and Sir James Gowans,** 1857.

Pioneer two-up and two-down cottages,
forerunners of the Colonies type (see below)
but better detailed.

ROSEMOUNT BUILDINGS,
Gardner's Crescent
W. Lambie Moffat, 1858.

A different approach to the problem of artisan
housing; big patterned brick quadrangle,
originally of 96 flats, with towers on the
corners: a gloomy northern—English urban
aesthetic (Moffat originally practised at
Doncaster). Tactfully rehabilitated by Roland
Wedgewood Associates, 1979-81, to produce
a more useful, cheerful and attractive place to
live.

273 ROYAL BOTANIC GARDEN,
Inverleith Row

Iron and glass Palm House 1858 by Robert
Matheson; small octagonal Palm House with
splendid cast iron spiral staircases set into the
stone buttresses 1834. Note also memorial by
Robert Adam (1778) to Linnaeus, pioneer of
plant classification, to rear of new glasshouses
by George Pearce of DoE (1965). Glasshouses
themselves a fine angular exercise in tension
structures, comprising a series of large,
connected houses, some two storey, covering
a wide span. New administrative offices
alongside are vaguely neo-classical in a pre-
cast way: not unlike Mussolini's E.U.R.
building, which Piacentini designed near
Rome in 1937. Monumental Herbarium by
R. Saddler of DoE (1960).

Wedgewood

Rosemount Buildings

PSA

Arboretum New Glass Houses

1858 Palm House

RCAHMS

74 LAMMERBURN, 10 Napier Road
Sir James Gowans, 1860.

Good example of the unique but hardly playful style of Gowans: a veritable banquet of stone designed within his personal system of modular proportion. The more exceptional Rockville, Gowans' own panelled and turreted house, was opposite at 3 Napier Road until its demolition in 1966.

75 SALISBURY GREEN HOUSE,
Pollock Halls, Dalkeith Road
John Lessels, 1860-67.

Baronial mansion grafted on to an earlier house. Good interior work—particularly the neo-classical pendentived drawing room painted by Charles Frechou of Paris. Note also **St Leonard's Hall** also by Lessels, 1869; including stencils by Thomas Bonnar.

76 THE COLONIES, Glenogle Road
1861.

The most unusual of several schemes of terraced flats and houses for artisans, built by the Edinburgh Co-operative Building Company: others can be found behind Haymarket, Hermitage, Abbeyhill, Leith, Lochend and off Slateford Road: some thousands of flats in total. Apparently parallel terraces of two storey houses: in reality upper flats and lower flats each entered from a different street. Later developments (e.g. Slateford) varied the pattern. Many now gentrified—a tribute to their inherent quality.

77 FETTES COLLEGE, East Fettes Avenue
David Bryce, 1862-1870.

One of Edinburgh's finest buildings and a masterly addition to its dull northern skyline.

Lammerburn

Colonies, Glenogle Road

Combines details from several French chateaux, notably Blois and Chenonceau, and its studied symmetry is at odds with its romantic appearance. From the side elevation, the massing of towers and turrets to the crescendo of the central spire is perhaps Bryce's most exhilerating composition. Note also the **Dining Hall**, Rowand Anderson, Kininmonth & Paul 1966: somewhat flat in comparison with its fantastic neighbour.

Fettes

McKean

38 Dick Place

Scott Robertson

Barclay Church

278 *ALBERT TERRACE*
1863.

A plain, classical terrace of Victorian date; in a secluded, almost rustic corner of Edinburgh, by vanished Tipperlinn village. A ditty ran:

> *Braid Burn towlies*
> *Morningside swine*
> *Tipperlinn's the bonnie place*
> *Where a' the leddies dine.*

279 *TENEMENTS,* Fountainbridge/corner Grove Street
F. T. Pilkington, 1864.

The Pilkington touch is unmistakeable and can transform even the most dour corner tenement block such as this into a Grimm fairy tale.

280 38 *DICK PLACE*
F. T. Pilkington, 1864.

Very original Romanesque house designed for himself. Semi-detached houses also by him at 48-50.

281 *BARCLAY CHURCH,* Bruntsfield Place
F. T. Pilkington, 1864.

Pilkington used stone as most people would use plasticine, and the resulting muscular. almost pagan exuberance of composition and detail of this major Edinburgh landmark inspires awe at the architect's energy and self-confidence. The spire is visible for miles. Restored by David Carr Architects.

282 *KINGSTON CLINIC,* Kingston Avenue
F. T. Pilkington, 1869.

Spectacularly weird Gothic mansion, dominated by a grand circular tower and entrance loggia. Lovely grounds (private).

McKean

Fountainbridge Tenement

283 *HOLY CORNER,* Morningside Road

A lot of churches, even for Edinburgh, at this road junction. Baptist (originally Free) Church by MacGibbon & Ross, 1872; Christ Church Episcopal in complicated French Gothic by Hippolyte Blanc, 1875; North Morningside in heavy neo-Norman by David Robertson, 1879, containing outstandingly rich collection of stained glass windows; and the puny Morningside United in Early Christian style by James McLachlan, 1927.

284 *BELGRAVE CRESCENT, BUCKINGHAM TERRACE, LEARMONTH TERRACE*
John Chesser, begun 1874, 1860 and 1874 respectively.

Grand Victorian terraces which, like those just across the Water of Leith valley, bring a touch of Glasgow to Edinburgh, gaining discretion and losing nerve in the process.

85 CONVENT OF THE SACRED HEART,
219 Colinton Road, Craiglockhart
Peddie & Kinnear, 1878-80.

Impressive late classical hydropathic. Sheltered Siegfried Sasson and Wilfred Owen in First World War.

86 NILE GROVE and HERMITAGE TERRACE
Sir George Washington Browne, 1880s

Picturesque free-style 'art suburb' development. Browne also designed the octagonal Braid Church. R. Rowand Anderson was 'feuing architect' (in control of layout and design) of the Braid Estate to the south but many houses are by other architects, e.g. 1 Cluny Gardens 1885 by John Kinross, 18 Corrennie Gardens 1897 by Sydney Mitchell.

87 JAMES GILLESPIE'S SCHOOL,
Marchmont Crescent
Robert Wilson, Edinburgh School Board Architect, 1882.

Schools by him and his successor Carfrae appear all over the city. Note nearby Boroughmuir annexe, overlooking Bruntsfield Links, by Carfrae (1903).

88 ST. MICHAEL'S CHURCH, east end of Slateford Road
John Honeyman, 1883.

A scholarly and adventurous Glasgow architect trying his hand in foreign territory.

89 BRUNTSFIELD PLACE (next to the Barclay Church)
T. P. Marwick, 1885.

Two elaborate, breathtaking, tenements designed as a renaissance palace. Further out, a suave range by G. Washington Browne at 131-151 (1888), and more by **Hippolyte Blanc** at 155-195 (1882). To the east, the bold baronial Bruntsfield Crescent is by the famous historians MacGibbon & Ross, 1870, leading to the intensive middle-class, turreted and gabled tenements which tramp all over Warrender and Marchmont.

90 ST. JAMES THE LESS,
Episcopal Church, Inverleith Row
Sir Rowand Anderson, 1888.

Quiet unfinished late Gothic exterior conceals impressive re-furnishing by Sir John J. Burnet from 1894 onwards and rich mural decoration in chancel by William Hole.

91 CRAIGLOCKHART PARISH CHURCH,
Craiglockhart Avenue
George Henderson, 1889 and 1908.

Scots Gothic with tower and spire of excellent profile.

Nile Grove

292 SCIENNES SCHOOL, Sciennes Road
Robert Wilson and J. A. Carfrae, c. 1899.

Flamboyant stone Flemish-style Board school. Note also adjacent Royal Hospital of Sick Children, in pompous English neo-Jacobean by Sir George Washington Browne.

293 WAVERLEY, 82 Colinton Road
Sir James Gowans.

Designed for pen-nib manufacturer in an area developed in the 1880s, all in a monumental version of Gowans' quirky style. **Redhall Bank Cottages,** off Lanark Road, built for quarrymen, are in his rustic manner: lavish, two storey terrace with exuberant roof details. Redhall Bank is worth a visit for other, more modern buildings, in an élite and secluded neuk.

Castellated terraces tramping through Marchmont

20th Century

McKean

Oswald Road

Scott Robertson

Ravelston Lodge

Royal Victoria Hospital Extension

294 24 OSWALD ROAD, Grange
John Kinross, c. 1900.

Designed en suite with 31-35 Mortonhall Road, Kinross living in 33; all c. 1900, Scots revival, but of a different kind from Lorimer's: rubble, not harled, with corbelled bays. They lack Lorimer's softness thus being more redolent of institutional revivalists.

295 RAVELSTON LODGE, Queensferry Road c. 1900.

Architect unknown. Distant echo of an English-style Arts and Crafts cottage, à la Voysey, recognisable by its thick, tapered chimney and long, sweeping roof.

296 GRANTON GAS-HOLDERS
Walter Herring, engineer, 1902.

The earliest, with graceful steel lattice construction, is 1902: the other two 1933 and 1967.

297 KINGS THEATRE, Leven Street
J. D. Swanston and J. Davidson, 1905-6.

Good but not brilliant Edwardian Baroque, very completely preserved. Lavish woodwork, plasterwork and glasswork.

298 BALNAGOWAN, Murrayfield Drive
Parker & Unwin, 1906.

Picturesque, white harled house with nicely placed windows by celebrated Arts and Crafts architects from England, best known for their work in Hampstead Garden Suburb and Letchworth Garden City.

299 ROYAL VICTORIA HOSPITAL,
Craigleith Road
Sydney Mitchell, 1906.

Main building of engaging free design, with Baroque doorpiece and slim tower reminiscent of Clough Williams Ellis's work a little later. English-style gatehouse with slate-hung upper floor faces Craigleith Road. Extended in 1968 by Alan Reiach, Eric Hall and Partners, in the form of a modern cottage hospital: three sided courtyards on a plinth, in well detailed brown brick and mono-pitched roofs.

300 SHIELDAIG, 24 Hermitage Drive
Sir Robert Lorimer, 1906.

Outstanding house in Scots 17th century manner with curvilinear gables.

01 ARCHEPISCOPAL CHAPEL,
42 Greenhill Gardens
R. Schultz Weir, 1907.

Greek byzantine exterior with copper dome, interior details mainly by William Frame, brought from Falkland House.

02 ST. PETER'S CHURCH, Falcon Avenue, Churchill
Sir Robert Lorimer, 1908.

Italian-Byzantine church with campanile and forecourt, built for the aesthetes Canon John Gray and André Raffalovich. Considered by his contemporaries to be Lorimer's most original building,

03 REDFORD BARRACKS, Colinton Road
Harry B. Measures, 1909-15.

Unfriendly, late Victorian imperial parade of towered and domed infantry and cavalry barracks.

04 GEOGRAPHICAL INSTITUTE,
12 Duncan Street
Harry Ramsay Taylor, 1910-11.

Monumental, two-storey symmetrical front with the chilling two-tier portico rescued from the demolition of the much larger frontispiece to Falcon Hall in Morningside.

05 FIRST CHURCH OF CHRIST SCIENTIST,
Inverleith Terrace
Ramsay Traquair, 1910-11.

Bold, vaguely Art-Nouveau church, neo-Romanesque, with transverse saddleback tower forming a pleasing composition against the Edinburgh skyline. Simple single-span interior.

St. Peter's Church

306 BOROUGHMUIR SCHOOL, Viewforth
John Carfrae, 1911.

Huge, swashbuckling Renaissance school with Byzantine trimmings.

Boroughmuir School

307 St ANNE'S CHURCH, St. Johns Road,
Corstorphine
P. MacGregor Chalmers, 1911-13.

Italian Romanesque. Other churches by this
master of Romanesque revival are St.
Columba's Blackhall (1899) and St. Luke's
East Fettes Avenue, 1907.

308 HOLY CROSS EPISCOPAL CHURCH,
Quality Street, Davidson's Mains
J. M. Dick Peddie, 1912.

Squat cruciform church with central tower,
stone slate roofs: a whiff of Armenia.
Compare to Arts and Crafts Church of
Scotland across the road, with stone mullions,
leaded windows, eaves, ivy and a timber bell
tower.

*309 UNIVERSITY OF EDINBURGH HALLS
OF RESIDENCE,* East Suffolk Road
Alan K. Robertson, begun 1914.

Large Lorimerian campus, completed by
Frank Wood 1925.

310 NORTHFIELD BROADWAY,
off Willowbrae Road
Reginald Fairlie, 1919.

Some of Edinburgh's first local authority
housing, designed with Reid & Forbes, who
designed the classical Royal High Primary
School in 1931. It is grand urban scenery of a
French scale: wide roads, elegant blocks of
stone and brick flats vaguely neo-classical in
character.

311 PIERSHILL SQUARE, Portobello Road
E. J. Macrae, City Architect, 1938.

By far the most distinctive council house
development in Edinburgh. Two tapering
squares of ruggedly baronial stone flats, with
all the grimly romantic trimmings. MacRae
was responsible for an enormous programme
of building within Old Edinburgh,
particularly the Grassmarket, Cowgate and
Candlemaker Row. Some of his best
buildings are in St. Leonard's 1934, where he
retained the street layout, included shops on
the ground floor, and made a studious
attempt to recapture the Scots vernacular.
His Piershill Square Scheme suffers because it
has lost its street character.

312 BRISTO BAPTIST CHURCH,
Queensferry Road
William Paterson, 1932

Plain L-shaped building on corner site, with
long low sweeping roof and Dutch gables.

313 REID MEMORIAL CHURCH,
Blackford Road
Leslie Grahame Thomson, 1933.

Lorimer-influenced Gothic church at major
crossroads; Surrounding cloistral buildings to
the east of a very high order. Proportions of
this complex are better than Lorimer often
achieved.

RCAHMS/Scottish Colorfoto

Reid Memorial Church

Inglis Stevens

Above: *Piershill Square* **Below:** *MacRae's earlier
housing in St Leonard's*

City of Edinburgh

Maybury Roadhouse

46a Dick Place

4 46a DICK PLACE
By and for **Sir William Kininmonth** of **Kininmonth & Spence**, 1933.

Small, white-rendered, private house in garden of neighbour; later extended. International modern on miniature scale. Usual contrast between curve and rectangle—typical roof-terrace and canopy. Unusual in that proportions are vertical and not horizontal, and timber windows instead of metal.

5 DOMINION CINEMA, Newbattle Terrace
Bowhill Gibson, 1936.

Edinburgh lacks a cinema of the panache to be found in London. The **Dominion** is a country cousin of the *moderne* style, with fins in stonework.

6 LISMHOR, 11 Easter Belmont Road.
Kininmonth & Spence, 1935.

Another Modern Movement house, on the West side of Edinburgh, with superb views. White render, corner windows and a circular chimney. Later extended.

317 RESTAURANT and PUB,
Maybury roundabout
Patterson & Broom, 1935.

1930s roadhouse: white curves, streamlined horizontals, metal strip windows, and oversailing canopies. Has considerable vulgar flair and deserves revitalisation.

Glenlockhart Bank

318 4 GLENLOCKHART BANK
George Lawrence, 1937.

White rendered house with many contemporary stylistic details, eg: L-shaped stair window, porthole and curved bay window to the drawing room.

H

Ravelston Gardens

**319 *RAVELSTON GARDENS,* Ravelston Dykes
Neil & Hurd, 1937.**

Three fine blocks of international-style flats
on butterfly plan, complete with roof gardens,
canopies and adjacent garages. Known
originally as the Jenners Flats, after their
managing agents.

**320 *HOUSE,* 409 Queensferry Road
MacTaggart & Mickel, 1937.**

Typical '30s *moderne* stylistic features—
metal, horizontally proportioned windows
going round corners etc., unfortunately
spoiled by the pitched roof. Set the pattern for
the post-war development of the Hillpark
area.

321 *THISTLE FOUNDATION SETLEMENT,*
Niddrie Mains Road
Lorimer & Matthew, 1950.

Robin Chapel and memorial homes for
disabled: now looking rather sad and
institutionalised. Rows of cream washed
cottages, red roofed with green window
frames, around the stone chapel. The
surrounding estate of Niddrie is typical of
early 1970s architecture; harled, array of
pitched roofs, and tall gables. Lack of variety,
colour and landscaping make it rather
forbidding.

409 Queensferry Road

322 *WEST PILTON CIRCUS*
City Architect, completed 1951.

In Vienna these houses would be painted
white and lived in by Professors: in
Edinburgh they plan to demolish them. Neat,
two storey blocks of flats with metal windows
and square chimneys in a cramped version of
garden city layout. Suffering from loss of
image, lack of maintenance, and cost-cutting
construction. Similar to houses in
Broomhouse Drive; but the latter are three-
storey, and lack the enlightened layout. Even
there, a simple paintwork scheme would work
wonders.

Maidencraig Court

Sighthill Health Centre

Western General Hospital

3 MAIDENCRAIG COURT,
Queensferry Road
Leslie Grahame MacDougall, 1953.

Attempt to give architectural form to a slab block of flats by curving it and placing diminutive (and rather weak) pediments above each staircase, with elegant balconies, a shallow copper roof, and an overall pleasing post-modern symmetry.

4 SIGHTHILL HEALTH CENTRE,
Calder Road
R. Gardner-Medwin, 1953.

Good exemplar of the period. Courtyard development, with main two-storey block on the north. The latter exhibits nice, typical details: entrance is under columns, the bay windows to the north have a jagged profile, and the central staircase is beautifully curved and lit. Shallow pitched roof originally clad in green copper: variegated repairs have practically transformed the roofscape to tartan.
Note adjacent Sighthill Hotel for *moderne* details of the late '30s.

325 WESTERN GENERAL HOSPITAL,
Crewe Road
1950s.

Centred on, but ignoring the old Poor House by Peddie and Kinnear (1867). A number of buildings, particularly the out-patients entrance, and the surgical, neurology and physiotherapy departments, clearly show their 1950s date, designed by South East Regional Hospital Board (architect John Holt). Period details everywhere: particularly the patent glazing, boxed out windows, canted balconies, timber-clad, shaped, roof structures, and the barrel vaulted roofs of the boilerhouse. Even the colour of the brick.

Avisfield

Clapperfield

Pollock Halls

326 AVISFIELD, Cramond Road North
1958, extended 1964 by **Morris & Steedman.**

Elegant, single-storey L-shaped house, of two
interlocking rectangles with oversailing flat
roofs. Stone wall encloses the other two sides
to complete the courtyard and provide, in
effect, a sheltered outdoor room.

327 ST. JOHN'S CHURCH,
Oxgangs Road North
Alan Reiach & Partners, 1958.

Simple, cottage-style, white church, with
interesting glass-panelled wall and boarded
ceiling.

328 CLAPPERFIELD, Old Mill Lane,
Nether Liberton
Stuart Renton for himself, 1959.

Single-storey architect's house, L-shaped with
a garage completing the symmetry:
monopitch roofs, white painted brick walls
inside out and out, contrasting with timber
windows, doors and ceilings. Alan Reiach
developed some of these ideas in his own,
nearby house, 5 Winton Loan, 1964.

329 POLLOCK HALLS OF RESIDENCE
(University of Edinburgh), Dalkeith Road
Rowand Anderson, Kinimonth & Paul,
1959.

Very stylish, Swedish influenced, courts of
pale brick, shallow green copper roofs, and
Swedish lanterns above the entrances. The
arcades on the interior show clear similarities
to Jesse Hartley's 1840s Albert Docks, in
Liverpool, which were published in the
Functional Tradition only a few years
previously.

30 CAERKETTON COTTAGES,
Firhill Crescent
M. J. Blanco White and A. Abbott, 1960.
Short terrace of yellow washed, red tiled,
cottages.

31 HOUSES, Gracemount Road
Eric Hall and Partners, 1963.
Small scheme whose profile strongly recalls
Arne Jacobsen's earlier houses in Soholm,
Denmark. An essay in contrasts: roof pitches,
rendered walls, brick walls and square,
slender chimneys.

32 SCOTTISH GAS HEADQUARTERS,
West Shore Road, Granton
Thomas Hughes (former Scottish Gas
architect). 1960s.
Smooth tinted glass and steel pavilions in
otherwise messy setting. Later additions by
James Parr and Partners. Note nearby
Trendcentre supermarket, off West Shore
Road, Reiach and Hall, 1978. Notable for its
bright, blue, pressed metal wall panels
derived from Milton Keynes factory
prototypes. Brightens a gloomy area.

Gracemount Road

33 KING'S BUILDINGS, Mayfield Road/
West Mains Road.

A technological, suburban campus for the
University: an architecturally incoherent
jungle of buildings modified by fine planting,
with one or two of interest to those prepared
to ensure the mess, as follows:—

School of Agriculture (Reiach and Cowan,
1960.) A large, hybrid scheme designed in
1948 and looks it. Raised to a different plane
by the protruding, curved roofs of the dining
room etc. **Department of Engineering
Lecture Theatre** (R. Gardner Medwin, with
Stevenson Young and Partners, 1961.)
Animal Breeding Research Headquarters
(Sir Basil Spence, Glover and Ferguson,
1962.) **Experimental Petrology** (Reiach and
Hall, 1968.) Single storey laboratories around
a courtyard, distinguished by their massive,
chamferred ventilation towers. **Boilerhouse,
Refectory and central facilities** (Michael
Laird and Partners, 1970-75.) Streamlined
development of curved, pre-cast wall units,
topped by a continuous, canted clerestorey,
itself dominated by a clutch of elegantly
tapered flues.

Kings Buildings **Above:** *School of Agriculture*
Below: *Refectory and Boiler House*

34 LIBERTON DAMS POLICE STATION,
Mayfield Road
Morris & Steedman, 1963.

One of a series of district stations: cosy single
storey building above car parking, flat roof
with copper fascia, and simple, neat
brickwork and redwood windows. In keeping
with the adoption by the constabulary of a
'low profile.'

Snoek

McKean

65 Ravelston Dykes Road

335 65/67 RAVELSTON DYKES ROAD
Morris & Steedman, 1963.

Pair of large, white, flat-roofed houses with upper drying balcony: living quarters above for sun and view, private quarters below. Open upper-floor can be subdivided or entirely open.

Snook

St. Crispen's School

Music School, George Watson's

336 SILVERKNOWES GOLF CLUB HOUSE
Alan Reiach & Partners, 1964.

Small pavilion set on hillside overlooking the Forth. A simple, elegant, somewhat domestic design principally of brick walls, board marked concrete, and timber roofs, with the main rooms on the first floor, for the view. A good exemplar of the design vocabulary of the time. Later extended by Campbell and Arnott.

337 ST. CRISPIN'S SCHOOL FOR HANDICAPPED CHILDREN,
Watertoun Road
Law and Dunbar Nasmith, 1964.

Elegant disposition of single and two-storey blocks of classrooms enclosing courtyards. The result is a crisp, cubist geometry, humanised by the use of brick structural walls, and redwood boarding.

338 MUSIC SCHOOL, George Watson's College,
Colinton Road
Michael Laird & Partners, 1964.

Distinguished by its bird-like timber, hyperbolic parabolic, roof; at end of Memorial building containing library and teaching rooms.

*Mary Erskine's School The roofs of Ravelston House
can be seen above left*

339 CHILDREN'S HOSPITAL UNIT,
Astley Ainslie Hospital, Grange Loan
Michael Laird & Partners, 1965.

Sizeable three storey hospital building of
some elegance: the vertical rhythm of
columns contrasts with horizontal emphasis of
the wards.

340 MARY ERSKINE SCHOOL FOR GIRLS,
Ravelston Dykes
Rowand Anderson Kininmonth and Paul,
1966.

A cubist influenced development of white-
harled, clean cut geometric shapes, neatly
dug into the grassy slopes of **Ravelston
House**; itself one of Edinburgh's grander
country houses of 1791, sporting a three-
storey castellated bow à la Culzean. Remains
of 17th century Old Ravelston House
adjacent.

Fair a Far Houses

341 PRINCES MARGARET ROSE HOSPITAL,
Clinical and nurses training units,
Frogston Road
Morris & Steedman, 1966.

There is a separate department on each floor,
the major feature being the specialized lecture
theatre, overlooking the plantation at rear.
The elegant, reflective, stepped profile
indicates location of the theatre auditorium.

342 FAIR A FAR HOUSING, Barnton
Philip Cocker Associates, 1966/73.

Mixed scheme of houses and flats for a co-
ownership housing association. Traditional
materials: brick and tile. See also nearby
scheme in **Southfield Avenue,** Barnton; a
scheme of 116 homes and flats, with rendered
walls and tiled roofs.

Princess Margaret Rose Hospital

J R Rock

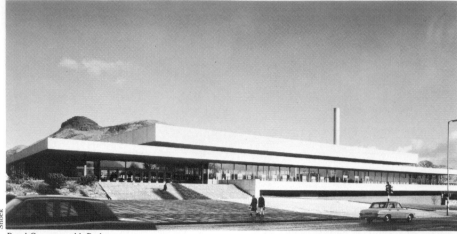

Snoek

Royal Commonwealth Pool

343 ROYAL COMMONWEALTH POOL,
Dalkeith Road
**Robert Matthew Johnson-Marshall &
Partners, 1967.**

An elegantly successful building containing
Olympic standard pool and two others, with
seating for 1700 spectators. Clean, horizontal
lines against the backdrop of Arthur's Seat,
the glazed entrance level acting as a **piano
nobile:** below, the structure is reinforced
concrete clad in dark engineering brick;
above, it is light exposed steelwork.

344 HOUSING, Craigmount Avenue North
Roland Wedgewood Associates, 1968.

Housing Society scheme of 110 houses and
flats with private gardens encircling a
protected communal garden at the centre.
Early use of *vernacular* elements such as
pitched roofs, gables and harled walls, all
contriving to reduce the apparent density of
the development. Treatment of parking, and
road frontage very much ahead of its time.

345 9 BURGESS TERRACE
**Ian G. Lindsay & Partners, (Ian Marshall),
1968.**

Private house for the architect himself. A
kinked two-storey building of painted
blockwork on a cramped garden site, whose
dark timberwork for doors and windows,
glass blocks, and massing make this one of
Edinburgh's most unusual houses of that
period.

346 69-85 RAVELSTON DYKES ROAD
Roland Wedgwood Associates, 1969.

Row of 9 private houses stepped down a
slope, overlooking R. R. Steedman-designed
communal garden and lochan. First floor
balconies with a horizontal timber emphasis
for the upper floor above a brick ground floor.

9 Burgess Terrace

69 Ravelston Dykes Road

Mortonhall Crematorium

Nuffield Transplantation Unit

47 MORTONHALL CREMATORIUM,
Howdenhall Road
Sir Basil Spence, Glover & Ferguson, 1967.

Two chapels linked by service block, in white concrete block. Derivative from Coventry in way that stained glass windows attract indirect light into the chapels. Interior is particularly good.

48 CRAIGSBANK CHURCH, Corstorphine
Rowand Anderson, Kininmonth & Paul,
1967.

Ambiguous, harled, almost windowless

building whose plain cubist shapes contrast with the dominant, Spanish-style, semi circular bell tower. More like a pilgrimage chapel than a community kirk.

349 NUFFIELD TRANSPLANTATION SURGERY UNIT, Western General Hospital, Crewe Road
Peter Womersley, 1968.

An expressive, highly sculptural, building in deep muddy yellow concrete: now staining rather sadly. One of the most overtly poetic modern buildings in Edinburgh.

Craigsbank Church

350 CHRISTIAN SALVESEN (MANAGERS) HEAD OFFICE, 50 East Fettes Avenue **Morris & Steedman,** 1969.

Neat courtyard development open on south corner: terraced into sloping site. Contains open plan offices with lecture and staff facilities.

351 WESTER HAILES
Sir Frank Mears and Partners, 1970s.

Gigantic, dense township with 4,800 houses, dominated by major peripheral roads. Some attempt at white-harled, circular-staircase Scots tradition. Development includes shopping, community and health centres. Similar in planning, separation of pedestrian and car routes, and concentration of public buildings, to a miniature New Town. Population 16,000.

352 MEADOWBANK STADIUM, London Road **City Architects' Department,** 1970.

Major 15,000 seat stadium linked to an intensively used Sports Centre, visually dominated by the gigantic cantilevered steel roof which protects over 8000 people from the climate.

Meadowbank Stadium

353 SCOTTISH AGRICULTURAL INDUSTRIES, off Ravelston Terrace **Roland Wedgwood Associates,** 1972.

H-shaped development of three and four storeys in bronze brick. Precise detailing of the windows and string-courses, gives the building satisfying proportions.

354 HOUSES, South Gyle Gardens **Edinburgh City Architects' Department,** 1974.

Development of 143 houses, each with a private garden, organised around four main courtyards on either side of a pedestrian spine. Harled, mono-pitch roofs, neither overtly folksy, nor urban in character.

Scottish Agricultural Industries

355 QUEEN MARGARET COLLEGE, Clerwood Terace **Andrew Renton,** 1973.

Competition winning design set into Corstorphine Hill. Pleasant collegiate layout, the design dominated by the white-metalled fenestration and the black horizontal facings. Bright new library and hexagonal **Social accommodation building**—same exterior, but more more colourfully exciting interior—by Simpson and Brown, 1977 and 1982.

South Gyle Gardens

56 RICCARTON CAMPUS, Heriot-Watt
University, Currie
Alan Reiach, Eric Hall and Partners,
1967-76.

University campus on a mature, country
estate. Consistent use of brown brick, white
concrete panels and olive-green metal
sheeting. As in most new universities, the
plan provides for covered, traffic free
pedestrian routes throughout the campus.
The most distinctive parts of the development
are the banded concrete and brick residences
beside the loch (vaguely similar to Churchill
College, Cambridge) and the Hugh Nisbet
building which contains the social facilities,
and a fine bay-windowed, coffered ceilinged,
pillared coffee room. The library is by Sir
Basil Spence, Glover and Ferguson.

57 EDINBURGH AIRPORT
Robert Matthew, Johnson-Marshall &
Partners, 1975.

Old building (now project terminal) by
Robert Matthew (1954). New building is a
popular U-shaped, linear building, with
suitably smooth styling: steel frame, dark
glass, and brown prefabricated metal panels.

Above: *Hugh Nisbet Building, Heriot-Watt campus*
Below: *Edinburgh Airport*

58 SCOTTISH WIDOWS ASSURANCE HQ,
Dalkeith Road
Sir Basil Spence, Glover and Ferguson,
1976.

Elephant proportioned dark glass hexagons
under the lee of Arthur's Seat. Stunning

landscaping on roof designed by Sylvia
Crowe. Main internal space is the Dining
Room with typical Spence fun with the
floating staircase. RIBA Award 1978.

Scottish Widows

Snock

359 SOUTH GYLE HOUSING
Robert Hurd & Partners, 1979.

Scottish neo-vernacular, speculative housing for Mactaggart and Mickel, with mini-tower houses, slates and orange pantiles in an industrial wilderness.

360 QUALITY STREET, Davidson's Mains
Ian G. Lindsay and Partners, 1979.

Speculative development of brown brick and timber terraced houses distinguished by projecting party walls which sweep down into the gardens.

361 SHELTERED HOUSING, Argyle Park Terrace
A. Campbell Mars (of Calthrop and Mars), 1981.

Tall L-shaped development overlooking the Meadows from the south. Brown brick walls and grey slate roof, with a bulky roof profile.

Davidson's Mains Houses

362 POST OFFICE SORTING OFFICE, Leith Walk (Brunswick Road)
Sir Basil Spence, Glover and Ferguson, 1982.

Great silver industrial shed in wriggly tin, with slender, scarlet chimneys, guard rails and escape doors. Interlocking north light gables and extraction ducts. Interior is large span shed with bright blue service trunking for diversion. The complex handles all mail from Edinburgh and the adjacent area.

Above: *Argyll Park.* **Below:** *GPO Sorting Offices*

McKean

Above: *Lloyds and Scottish Finance* **Right:** *Cameron Crescent flats*

363 LLOYDS AND SCOTTISH FINANCE LTD.,
Orchard Brae
J. & F. Johnston and Partners, 1981.

Sleekly horizontal extension behind the main building, with more than a touch of ziggurats. Clean contrast between brilliant white walls and dark strip windows.

364 FLATS, Moncrieffe Terrace
Groves-Raines and Spens, 1979-82.

Bright scarlet balconies, blue wire mesh balustrades, and facetted windows set in honey-coloured concrete blocks. The main staircase is glazed from top to toe, and ribbed with horizontal, scarlet timberwork of agricultural proportions.

365 FLATS, Cameron Crescent
Nicholas Groves-Raines, 1983.

Staggering block of flats whose dominant aesthetic is North County Victorian industrial: modified by 1930's horizontally in fenestration, and patterned cream and brown brickwork.

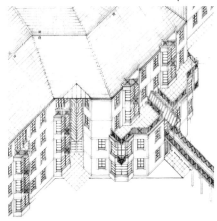

366 NATIONAL LIBRARY EXTENSION,
Causewayside
Sir Basil Spence, Glover and Ferguson.
Unbuilt

A largely, highly serviced book store which will be enlivened by projecting glazed staircases and solid lift shafts with triangulated tops.

National Library Extension

Postscript

Charles McKean

Edinburgh's architectural wealth is staggering—as much for its less well-known pre 1700 buildings as for its more celebrated Georgian developments. The consequence of such an inheritance is that a very high proportion of architectural work in Edinburgh has been in the field of restoration or rehabilitation., Virtually every building in this **Guide** has undergone some form of architectural treatment within the last 40 years. Consequently, for the work of current day architects in Edinburgh, one often has to be looking at historic buildings. Unfortunately, the presence of such a fine architectural past can intimidate good new design. In comparison to the major redevelopment explosion of the 1960s, buildings of the '70s were more timid. and now only are we beginning to see a new stirring. So far, therefore, there are few examples of genuinely urban modern architecture in Edinburgh, although there is a growing quantity of brand new, quasi-rural quasi-traditional architecture even as close to the centre as Stockbridge.

New buildings in Edinburgh must respect the City's urban scale and their relationship with adjacent buildings, but that is no reason for flabbiness. We have travelled a long way since the City gave over its major new development—the New Town—to an open architectural competition: and an even longer way since the City decided to back an unknown twenty-two year old architect, James Craig, as the winner. Furthermore, there is more aesthetic control now than ever before in Edinburgh's history; yet the onlooker may wonder what genuine advances in Edinburgh's architecture there is to show for it. The essence of Edinburgh is architectural vigour in a fine setting. If architectural competitions are to be the only way of regaining that vigour, let us have more of them. The alternative is stagnation.

References

Many books have obviously been consulted in the preparation of this **Guide,** whose format precludes the normal method of reference.

The most significant were: *Early Travellers in Scotland,* Hume Brown; *The Making of Classical Edinburgh,* A. J. Youngson; *The Eye is Delighted,* Maurice Lindsay; *Sir James Gowans,* Duncan McAra; *Memorials of His Time,* Lord Cockburn; *Lorimer and the Edinburgh Craft Designers,* Peter Savage; *Baronial and Ecclesiastical Antiquities of Scotland,* R. W. Billings; *The Castellated and Domestic Architecture of Scotland,* McGibbon and Ross; *The City of Edinburgh,* RCAHMS; *Edinburgh in the days of our Grandfathers,* James Gowans; *Mr David Bryce,* Exhibition Catalogue; *In Praise of Edinburgh,* Rosaline Masson; *Biographical Dictionary of British Architects, 1600-1840,* Howard Colvin.

Index of Architects